OUTSTANDING

AMERICAN

STATESMEN

OUTSTANDING

AMERICAN

STATESMEN

edited by Russell H. Lucas

Lectures by: William Henry Harbaugh

Arthur S. Link

Frank Freidel

Alfred I. Chandler, Jr.

SCHENKMAN PUBLISHING COMPANY, INC.

CAMBRIDGE, MASSACHUSETTS

TABLE OF CONTENTS

Preface vii

PART 1   THEODORE ROOSEVELT
              by William Henry Harbaugh . . .   1

PART 2   WOODROW WILSON AND AMERICAN
              TRADITIONS
              by Arthur S. Link 17

PART 3   FRANKLIN D. ROOSEVELT: THE
              QUEST FOR SECURITY
              by Frank Freidel 34

PART 4   DWIGHT D. EISENHOWER – THE
              TRAINING AND THE TASKS
              by Alfred D. Chandler, Jr. 57

PREFACE

The papers in this series on four of the greatest American statesmen of the Twentieth Century were written by the four recognized authorities respectively on these statesmen. Professor William H. Harbaugh of the University of Virginia is the author of the full length biography of Theodore Roosevelt and the editor of a volume of selections from forty-one volumes of Roosevelt's Works, letters, and addresses. Professor Arthur S. Link of Princeton University is the author of five volumes, thus far, of the definitive eight volume biography of Woodrow Wilson and the editor of a forty volume edition of Wilson's Works, papers and letters, five of which have thus far been published. Professor Frank Freidel, Jr. of Harvard University is the author of three volumes, thus far, of a definitive nine volume biography of Franklin D. Roosevelt. Volume IV will be published in 1970. Professor Alfred D. Chandler, Jr., Chairman of the Department of History at The Johns Hopkins University, is the editor of a twelve volume edition of General Eisenhower's personal letters and papers. The first four volumes should be published in 1970.

Any reader generally familiar with the writings of these scholars bearing on their respective subjects in the series will be impressed with the skill with which they have here condensed their views so as to provide a well balanced conception of the political principles and policies of the respective statesmen and how they met the challenges provided by the rise of technology and the organization of industry on a large scale in this century. The rise of technology and organization of large scale industry has laid the basis among other things for great and ultimately devastating military power calling for a global viewpoint on the part of national leaders and also of great numbers of ordinary citizens if the country and indeed mankind is to survive. The four papers here presented, then, trace the evolution in the attainment of this viewpoint by these statesmen.

These papers were originally lectures arranged by the Society of Mayflower Descendants in Michigan for delivery at consecutive annual meetings of the Society from November 1965 to November 1968 inclusive during the terms of office of Russell H. Lucas, Past Governor, and Senator Gilbert E. Bursley, Present Governor of the Society. The William Lyon Phelps Foundation of Detroit participated in the support of the project. The educators and statesmen whose counsel and influence enlisted the interest of the four distinguished historians comprised Professor Samuel Miller Brownell of Yale University, formerly Commissioner of Education in the Eisenhower Administration and formerly Superintendent of Schools in Detroit; Ambassador Shelby Cullom Davis, long Chairman of the Alumni Advisory Committee on history at Princeton, and a generous benefactor of its History Department; and Dr. Walter D. Wagoner, Executive Director of The Boston Theological Institute of Cambridge, Mass., and formerly a colleague of Dr. Link on the faculty of Northwestern University. Professor Brownell is a member of the Society of Mayflower Descendants in Michigan. Ambassador Davis is a member of the New York Society of Mayflower Descendants. Dr. Wagoner is a trustee of The William Lyon Phelps Foundation.

THEODORE ROOSEVELT

By William Henry Harbaugh

One reason, I suspect, we are assembled here tonight is that we accept Santayana's dictum: "Those who do not remember the past are condemned to repeat it." More specifically, we seek –, in the manner of all men in all ages, wisdom, guidance, and inspiration from the writings and deeds of one of our great men. A large order in any circumstance, this is an almost impossible order in Theodore Roosevelt's. For he remains in death as he was in life – an extraordinarily, almost uniquely controversial man. There is hardly more agreement today than there was forty-nine years ago when he died on the real nature of his character, the quality of his presidential administrations, and his influence upon his times.

Thus some historians have portrayed him as a perennial adolescent, as a crypto fascist, or a sheer opportunist. Others have viewed him as a sophisticated conservative, a moderate liberal, or a dedicated reformer. Some have contended that he had little constructive impact upon American history; some, even, that his influence was essentially destructive. Others – and I confess I fall into this category – have argued that his impact upon men and events was both considerable and constructive; that he took America into the world in foreign policy and into the twentieth century in domestic policy. And still other historians – usually of the behaviorist school – have held that he simply mirrored his times. He was, they say, in no sense responsible for forming the social forces that produced the Progressive Movement; if he hadn't harnessed them, someone else, presumably La Follette, would have.

I shall return to some of those interpretations in a few minutes. Meanwhile, let's look briefly at Theodore Roosevelt the man as he revealed himself and as some of his contemporaries saw him.

1

"I have come to the conclusion," T.R. wrote the President of Cornell University in 1900, on the eve of his election as Vice President, "that I have mighty little originality of my own. What I do is try to get ideas from men whom I regard as experts along certain lines, and then try to work out those ideas." Not long afterward he explained himself further to one of the G.O.P.'s machine bosses: "As for my impulsiveness and my alliance with labor agitators, social philosophers, taxation reformers and the like, ... I want to be perfectly sane. . . But I do have a good deal of fellow feeling for our less fortunate brother, and I am a good deal puzzled over some of the inequalities in life, as life now exists. . . All I want to do is cautiously to feel my way to see if we cannot make the general conditions of life a little easier, − a little better."

Flashes of self-revelation like those testify eloquently to Gifford Pinchot's assertion that Roosevelt had "true humility of mind." As he so disarmingly confessed, he was neither an original nor a profound thinker. His works are almost barren of the assertions of first principles that give enduring interest to the writings of the Founding Fathers and that give nobility to Jefferson, Lincoln, and Wilson. Yet, T.R.'s writings are fraught with human interest and practical wisdom. No American President was so widely, and in certain areas, so deeply read. No President enjoyed literature more, wrote history as well, or understood the world of nature better. Robert Frost called him one "of our kind." Van Wyck Brooks considered him "a man of genius." And the professional naturalist who accompanied him to Africa in 1909 said that "I constantly felt while with him that I was in the presence of the foremost naturalist of our time, as indeed I was."

For all the strident egotism and ruthlessness that alienated many of his contemporaries and continues to alienate many historians, T.R.'s personality was uniquely appealing. Generous, considerate, and fairminded, he valued men for what they were. "He was different from anybody that I had ever met," his Maine hunting guide recalled. "He didn't look for a brilliant man when he found me." Scores of intimates have remarked on his graciousness and seemingly inborn courtesy. And even his arch-enemy, Woodrow Wilson, confessed that Roosevelt had "charmed" him. "There is," he said, "a sweetness about him that is very compelling. You can't resist the man."

The scion of an old Dutch mercantile family long prominent in New York City's affairs, Roosevelt was inculcated as a matter of course with a belief in philanthropy, noblesse oblige, and civic responsibility. His father had an especially powerful influence upon him. "He was the only man I ever feared," he once said. "I realize more and more every day," T.R. wrote in his diary some months after his father's death in 1878, "that I am as much inferior to father morally and mentally as physically." From him, apparently, T.R. derived his sense of justice. At first, to be sure, his concept of justice was retributive; he was concerned essentially, that is, with punishment. Yet because he was an intelligent and scientifically-minded man no less than a moralistic man, he gradually came to conceive of justice in distributive terms as well. The changes in his attitude toward labor and the under-privileged are revealing of this.

When Roosevelt entered the New York Legislature in 1882 at the age of twenty-three, he carried most of the prejudices of his class with him. He was contemptuous of recent immigrants. He regarded the poor as slothful, the rich as industrious and virtuous. And he subscribed uncritically to the laissez-faire beliefs of his Harvard professors and family friends. For him as for them, the laws of economics were fixed and inviolable. As late as his third term he dismissed a bill to reduce the working hours of streetcar conductors to twelve — (to twelve, not from twelve) — per day with the shibboleth that it was no more possible to alter the iron laws of economics than to repeal the law of gravity.

Yet his three terms in the legislature were also marked by his first breakthrough, — this on a bill to regulate tenement workshops in which Samuel Gompers engaged his interest. "The respectable people I knew were against it," T.R. recalled, "and it was contrary to the principles of political economy of the laissez-faire kind." Furthermore, "the businessmen who spoke to me about it shook their heads and said that it was designed to prevent a man doing as he wished and as he had a right to do with what was his own." Nevertheless, he gave it full and effective support, and thereafter his concern for distributive justice steadily deepened. By the time the Progressive Movement reached its height, he was even a proponent of unemployment insurance, public works programs, and a social security system.

Roosevelt's concern with justice also had a marked impact upon his attitude toward law. Like most conservatives (and you'll note that I have called him a conservative; I intend to come back to that shortly), like most conservatives, he was obsessed by the need for order; as Police Commissioner of New York City he prosecuted criminals relentlessly. But unlike many men who call themselves conservatives, he insisted that the law should be enforced against rich and poor alike. During his presidency, he repeatedly lashed the judiciary for using the injunction as a means of stopping strikes and thwarting the organization of labor unions. He perceived the nature of what is today called "white-collar" crime. Again and again, in a series of messages aptly termed "the most radical ever sent in to Congress to that time,"he flailed the courts for failing "to stop" what he called "the abuses of the criminal rich." Again and again he condemned juries for failing to impose prison sentences on reputable businessmen who had broken the law.

Now, a moment ago I labelled T.R. a conservative, and several minutes ago I said that many historians have called him a sophisticated conservative. And in between I termed a series of his messages radical. What do I mean? Certainly little that I've said to this point denominates him a conservative in the accustomed — and I say thoughtless — use of the term.

First, his radicalism: He sometimes acted radically, but he was in no sense a radical. He believed in private property, in capitalism, in modified form; he never sought to alter the fundamental structure of American society. His economic thought was Hamiltonian, diluted, or perhaps I should say enriched, by the compassion of Lincoln. He understood the importance of capital formation; he knew there could be little improvement of wages without increases in production. Like Hamilton, moreover, he had a national view of the economy. But unlike Hamilton, he did not believe that business had the right to fix the destiny of the nation. Business — and he felt the same way, of course, about labor, though he did not flail it as often because it was so weak and exploited at the time — must be made to fulfill its social responsibilities. This was to be done in three ways: First, the most anti-social trusts were to be dissolved under the Sherman Anti-trust Act. Ironically, for T.R. still lives in the popular mind as the great "trust-buster", he regarded that as the least efficacious solution. As President, he instituted only about half as many anti-trust proceedings as Taft. Second, labor was to be upgraded to the point that it would constitute a countervailing power to business. He did not use that term; but that is what his policy of encouraging the formation of industry-wide unions amounted to. Third, the government, representing all the people – as defender that is of the commonwealth – was to be above both business and labor. This meant federal laws – many of them: The Hepburn railroad regulation act, the Pure Food and Drug Act, the Employers' Liability Act, and an extraordinarily creative series of conservation measures. It also meant a drastic transformation in the prevailing view of states', as opposed to federal, rights. T.R. had faced this forthrightly in his first annual message to Congress in 1901:

> When the Constitution was adopted, at the end of the Eighteenth Century, no human wisdom could foretell the sweeping changes, alike in industrial and political conditions, which were to take place at the beginning of the Twentieth Century. At that time it was accepted as a matter of course that the several states were the proper authorities to regulate, so far as this was then necessary, the comparatively insignificant and strictly localized corporate bodies of the day. The conditions are now wholly different and wholly different action is called for.

Seven years later, in words that cast a long shadow over the Republican future and give a telling insight into why T.R. stormed out of the G.O.P. and formed the Progressive Party in 1912, his theme was the same. The workingman, he declared, should be guaranteed "a larger share of the wealth." The corporations, he charged, were using the "appeal to the old doctrine of States' rights" as a "cover" in their fight against "adequate control and supervision."

Manifestly, he had failed to convert the old-line conservatives. The *New York Commercial and Financial Chronical* expressed a typical Old Guard reaction when it complained that if a fraction of Roosevelt's recommendations were put into law "they would commit the country to a course of new experiments and make over the face of social creation." But the *New York Sun,* I'm gratified to report was slightly more optimistic. By March 4, 1909, it assured its readers, "the seven-year flood of words" would be at last dried up.

Against this sketchy outline of T.R.'s advocacy of what is today called variously the welfare state, the regulatory state, or the mixed economy, I would like to focus for a moment on the assertion, alluded to earlier, that T.R. was fundamentally a sophisticated conservative rather than a true liberal or progressive. In one sense, that is, I think, a fair characterization. At the time, the conditions of life of millions upon millions of workingmen and their families were relatively as bad as those of the Negroes today, except of course for the stigma of race. There was probably more crime in the streets of certain ghettoes than there is today – that's an impressionistic judgment formed when I was doing research on Roosevelt's police commissionership in the 1890's; there is no hard data. There was certainly more real violence, by which I mean shootings and killings, than there is today – this because of a system of labor relations lasting until the 1930's which pitted armed company guards and sometimes special armies of Pinkertons against union organizers. (Most of those Victorian Gothic armories found in every large city of the land were built and paid for, you know, by men of substance who feared revolution in the last quarter of the 19th century.)

Roosevelt the conservative perceived this and feared it. Roosevelt the social thinker, the experimentalist, the sophisticated conservative and the man of action concluded that the way to avert revolution was to strike at the causes of revolution just as many thoughtful men, some of them the business leaders of this era, have similarly concluded today. He would, and did, put down rioters. But he never regarded that as a satisfactory solution. Almost without exception, his trust was constructive.

Insofar as Roosevelt was driven into reform by his fear of upheaval from below, he was, surely, a sophisticated conservative rather than a pure progressive. His object, clearly, was to preserve, to *conserve* if you will, our institutions by adapting them to the changes wrought by our transformation from an agrarian to an industrial economy. In degree, therefore, those who label him a sophisticated conservative are right. But only in degree.

Elihu Root, who was in truth a sophisticated conservative, graphically delineated this side of T.R. to a group of business and financial leaders in 1904. Alarmed by T.R.'s prosecutions and threatened prosecutions of the trusts, distrustful of his already advancing drive to regulate the railroads and other big business, they were attacking him as "unsafe" for business. Root replied:

> He is not safe for the men who wish govern-
> ment to be conducted with greater reference to
> campaign contributions than to the public good.
> He is not safe for the men who wish to draw the
> President of the United States off into a corner
> and make whispered arrangements, which they
> dare not have known by their constituents. But I
> say to you that he has been . . . the greatest
> conservative force for the protection of property
> and our institutions in the city of Washington.
> There is a better way to deal with labor, and to

keep it from rising into the tumult of
the . . . mob than by starving it, or by corrupting
its leaders . . . That way is that capital shall be
fair . . . fair to the consumer, fair to the laborer,
fair to the investor; that it shall concede that the
laws shall be executed . . .

No student of Roosevelt's career will quarrel with that
analysis; indeed, the pro-Roosevelt scholars and the anti-
Roosevelt scholars invariably use it. Yet, I ask, is it really
proper to classify T.R. with other sophisticated conservatives, men like Henry Cabot Lodge or Mark Hanna? I think
not. What distinguished him from them is this: They
tended to "stand pat" until the external pressures became
truly threatening. T.R. became morally indignant when
confronted with injustice; they remained largely indiffer-
ent. T.R. would become intellectually involved in the
reform itself – in its intrinsic social and economic merits –
and would make it a part of the corpus of his affirmative
beliefs; they would view it as a necessary evil. Above all
else, certainly, it was this positive accent that separated
Roosevelt from his sophisticated conservative consorts, the
real proponents of strategic retreat. His goal was justice.
He wanted not only to preserve, but to strengthen. He
wanted a more just and a less privileged America; they
wanted a more orderly America. He wanted the substance
of reform; they wanted the shadow. Surely the conclusion
is inescapable: T.R. was at once a conservative, a sophisticated conservative, and a committed progressive.

All three are implicit, and to some extent explicit, in his
attitude toward minority groups. In 1906, for example, he
appointed the merchant, Oscar Straus, Secretary of Com-
merce. Straus thus became the first Jew ever to sit in a
presidential cabinet. Why did T.R. appoint him? – partly
because it was good politics; partly because he wanted to

prevent Jews in general from becoming alienated or
disaffected; and partly because he deemed it a matter of
simple justice. "I grow extremely indignant at the attitude
of coarse hostility to the immigrant," T.R. explained to
the Protestant editor, Lyman Abbott:

> I have one Catholic in my Cabinet and have had
> another, and now I have a Jew in the Cabinet;
> and part of my object in each appointment was
> to implant in the minds of our fellow-Americans
> of Catholic or of Jewish faith, or of foreign
> ancestry or birth, the knowledge that they have
> in this country just the same rights and oppor-
> tunities as everyone else.

With your indulgence – for time is running on – I
should like now to make some comments on T.R.'s
conduct of foreign policy. Here, I suggest, is a record
literally riddled with ironies.

T.R. came to the presidency as an imperialist – as a
man convinced that empire was one of the hallmarks of
greatness, and that America's future welfare was actually
dependent on a heavy trade with the Far East in general and
with China in particular. But he left office convinced, first,
that there were practical limits to expansion and that the
United States had exceeded them in acquiring the Philippines; and, second, that the dream of a lucrative Far
Eastern trade was unrealistic, that the Open Door could
not be maintained, and that we should regard Japan's
aspirations to preeminence in the Far East as legitimate.

Nor were those the only ironies. T.R. came to the
presidency as a war-lover and a war-maker, but left it as a
kind of peace-broker – one who had contributed to
averting war over Morocco in 1905; one whose mediation
of the Russo-Japanese War that same year won him the
Nobel Prize. With almost rythmic regularity he had

appeared as a warhawk and peacemaker, as an ultra-nationalist and internationalist. He acted with impetuosity and with restraint, with bluster and with sensitivity, with force and with a spirit of accommodation. He wrote of "speaking softly and carrying a big stick" — and he sometimes did just that. Yet at other times he spoke loudly and carried no more than a twig.

Beneath those contradictory actions and statements, lay three principles: (1) self-defense was the first imperative of organized society; (2) the interests of highly advanced people took precedence over those of backward people, and (3) advanced people were morally obligated to support the onward march of civilization. Only in the light of these convictions can T.R.'s glorification of the warrior and the apparent contradictions between his domestic and foreign policies be understood.

Often, of course, extraneous factors such as his lust for military glory distorted his overall view. From his adolescence to his old age, he strained to prove himself by feats of physical courage and daring. More than once in the 1880's and 1890's he called for war in the ill-concealed hope that he might lead troops in battle — against Germany, against Mexico, against England, against almost anybody. And when, in 1898, he actually got his chance to fight, he confessed that he was going to war because it would enable him to cut his "little notch on the stick that stands as a measuring rod in every family."

Against that backdrop, I turn briefly to the application of T.R.'s principles to Latin America. Colombia, of which the state of Panama was part, was in T.R.'s view a backward nation. It had the temerity to refuse to accept the terms we laid down for the sale of Panama. Accordingly, T.R. had no moral compunction over — how shall I phrase it? — let us say acquiescing in — an externally financed (and fomented) revolution against Colombia by Panama. We organized this new nation – and I am putting it as mildly as it can be put – with undue haste and quickly made arrangements to acquire the ten mile strip through which the Panama Canal was later built.

Unquestionably, the Panama Canal benefited the United States and much of the world in that it expedited international trade. Yet, because T.R. acted with improper haste – he wanted, among other things, to build up a record to campaign on in 1904 – because he acted insensitively, and because he conspired to violate another country's sovereignty, he created a legacy of ill-will that survives in Colombia to this day.

Having acquired the Canal Zone, T.R. evolved from the principle of national security a new formula to protect it – the Roosevelt Corollary to the Monroe Doctrine. This came out of our intervention in the Dominican Republic in 1904. The Republic was threatened by the French and Italians for non-payment of debts; its President requested T.R. to intervene before they took military action. Reluctantly, he did so. "I have," he said, "about the same desire to annex it as a gorged boa constrictor might have to swallow a porcupine wrong-end-to." He then formalized the policy by stating that the United States assumed the right to interfere in the internal affairs of Latin American nations – something the original Monroe Doctrine had not assumed – in the event of "brutal wrong-doing" or "impotence."

Historians still differ in their evaluation of the policy of intervention T.R. thus instituted. In 1934 T.R.'s distant cousin, F.D.R., abrogated the Roosevelt Corollary as a good-will gesture. Yet the interventions continue. Some historians hold that the policy has contributed substantially to our national security; others suggest that because its implementation has almost invariably resulted in propping up unpopular and reactionary regimes we will reap the whirlwind when Latin America finally explodes in revolutionary violence.

T.R.'s most skillful, consummate, and responsible diplomacy occurred, I think, in the Far East. But again, note the irony. Aside from his lust for combat, the driving force behind T.R.'s desire to fight Spain in 1898 was his belief that it was in the American interest to drive Spain out of Cuba and the New World, and that it was in our interest to acquire the Philippines. By the same logic, of course, Roosevelt also supported the Open Door Notes, the objectives of which were not the welfare of China, but rather the prevention of Japan, Russia, and several European powers closing us out of the China trade.

Soon after he became President in September, 1901, T.R. perceived that Japan was destined to emerge as a major power in the Far East. By 1905 he had concluded that Japan should be encouraged to become a stabilizing force there on the theory that America's stake in the region would best be served by accepting the new realities. This meant acceptance of Japan's decision to impose herself on Korea. Elihu Root later explained why: "Many people are still angry because we did not keep Japan from taking Korea, There was nothing we could do except fight Japan; Congress wouldn't have declared war and the people would have turned out the Congress that had." T.R., in short, had comprehended the limits of American power. Nor was this an isolated incident. As T.R. also said when asked to intervene in Russia on behalf of the Jews and in Turkey on behalf of the Armenians: "it is a literal, physical impossibility to interfere under penalty of making this nation ridiculous and of aggravating . . . the fate of those for whom we interfere . . . unless there was intention to back up the words by an appeal to arms."

As the years passed, T.R. continued his policy of accommodation toward the Japanese. In 1908, in fact, he even agreed to recognize that she had a special interest in Manchuria. Meanwhile, in perhaps the greatest irony of his career, he termed the Philippines "our heel of Achilles" because of the impossibility of defending them. Then, two years after he left the presidency, he almost completely repudiated his earlier views on the Far East. The United States, he wrote President Taft, should abandon commercial aspirations in Manchuria. Japan's main interests, he said, were on the Continent. A successful war over Manchuria "would require a fleet as good as that of England, plus an army as good as that of Germany." The 'open door' policy in China was an excellent thing . . . but, it completely disappears as soon as a powerful nation determines to disregard it, and is willing to run the risk of war rather than forego its intention."

What, then, can we say of T.R.'s legacy in foreign policy in conclusion? Only this: he has left one legacy to the general public and a rather different one to historians. In the popular imagination, T.R. was a two-fisted, chest-thumping, trigger-happy flag-waver who stood for the assertion of American rights come what would. He was and is the incarnation of a militant nationalism that believes America is and always has been in the right; or, to put it another way, that believes whatever is *is* right simply because it is American.

The historian's image of T.R. is more complex. He sees all the above in T.R. − especially during his pre-presidential and post-presidential careers. In 1916, you will recall, T.R. even wanted us to go to war against Mexico. But the historian also sees a man who acted maturely and responsibly, except for the Panama affair, under the awesome burden of the presidency. He sees a

man who fulfilled international responsibilities in the
Moroccan and Russo-Japanese War crises; who had the
wisdom and perception to recognize the practical limits of
American power; and who sounded the first clear warning
against involvement in a land war in Asia. But the
historian's image, obviously, is not the one that has come
down through the years.

On the domestic side it is different. As Stanley M.
Isaacs, one of the young men who marched to Armageddon with T.R. in 1912 and who later served for years as
the conscience of New York City's council — and it needed
a conscience — once said to me:

> I doubt if anyone today can realize the
> personal inspiration that came from direct con-
> tact with T.R. or can appreciate the fervor that
> animated those of us who shared in the early
> Progressive Party years. T.R. gave us new goals, a
> broad purpose — faith in our conntry's ideals
> and willingness to press forward along lines we
> knew to be right, never willing to compromise
> where a vital moral issue was at stake, and
> confidence in the ultimate success of justice and
> sound ideas, provided they were pressed with
> courage and a disregard of personal
> consequences.

Mr. Isaac's evaluation, manifestly, is a subjective one.
Yet, in a certain sense, it is also an objective one.
Historians know from the testimony of numbers of men
more or less like him that T.R. had an extraordinary
influence on those who knew him just as they know, to
use an example familiar to this audience, that William
Lyon Phelps had an extraordinary influence on hundreds
upon hundreds of students at Yale. What they don't know,
or rather what they cannot measure, is the precise degree

of that influence.

On that note and with one last plea for your indulgence, I close with what is and remains my own evaluation of T.R.

"He was the first President-reformer of the modern industrial era — the first to concern himself with the judiciary's massive bias toward property, with the mal-distribution of wealth, and with the subversion of the democratic process by businessmen and their spokesmen in Congress; the first to comprehend the conservation problem in its multiple facets, the first to set forth a broad regulatory program for capital, and the first to encourage, however cautiously, the growth of labor unions. He was, in sum, the first President who both understood and reacted constructively to the problems created by the rise of a business civilization. His militance and his militarism will prevent him from ever being truly revered; his solid achievements, magnetic leadership and warm human qualities will assure him the begrudged respect of some and the unqualified affection of most."

WOODROW WILSON AND AMERICAN TRADITIONS

By Arthur S. Link

First, Mr. Chairman, permit me to thank you for your introduction. I am honored and delighted to be here tonight, speaking to this distinguished audience and participating in this series sponsored by the Society of Mayflower Descendants in the State of Michigan. I also want to pay tribute to the organizer and prime force behind these lectures, Mr. Russell H. Lucas.

A man of very serious mien walked to the stands outside the east front of the Capitol on Tuesday, March 4, 1913, to take the oath as twenty-eighth President of the United States. He was Woodrow Wilson, born in Staunton, Virginia, on December 28 or 29, 1856, educated at Davidson College and Princeton University, trained in law at the University of Virginia, and prepared for a career in teaching and scholarship in history and political science at The Johns Hopkins University. He had taught, from 1885 to 1902, successively at Bryn Mawr College, Wesleyan University in Connecticut, The Johns Hopkins, and Princeton University. Elected as thirteenth president of Princeton in 1902, he had taken leadership in transforming that venerable college into a distinguished university. Later embroiled in a bitter controversy with the Dean of the Graduate School, Andrew F. West, Wilson had escaped the troubled Princeton scene by accepting nomination for the governorship of New Jersey in the summer of 1910.

Elected forty-third Governor of New Jersey in that year, he had gone on from one triumph to another to capture the Democratic presidential nomination and then the presidency itself in 1912.

The man who was inaugurated on that March morning in 1913 was privileged to steer the American helm of state during eight of the most critical years of the modern epoch. The period of his tenure in the White House, 1913–1921, was a time when the American people, through their leaders, laid the foundations of a modern political economy. Abroad, these years were a time of revolutionary upheaval, of cataclysmic world war, and of fundamental shifts in the international balance of power that threatened to destroy altogether the foundation of the world community.

The circumstances and events of his presidential tenure were such that Woodrow Wilson could not have escaped playing an important role and achieving a certain greatness even had he been a second-rater with a passion for obscurity. But Wilson was a man of formidable intelligence and education, and a strongly-motivated activist whose determination to play a leading role in affairs was reinforced by the deep conviction that God had called him to the tasks at hand. Thus events and personality interacted, and Wilson's opportunities to contribute to American traditions were far larger than those given to most American statesmen.

In thinking about what I should say tonight, I have been somewhat overborne by the awesome dimensions of my task. It would be difficult enough to comment adequately upon Wilson's contributions to our domestic political traditions. But Woodrow Wilson was not content with one important career. He had three careers in addition to his career in domestic politics — as an historian and political scientist, as a teacher and university president, and, most important, as a diplomatist and builder of an organized international community. And so I trust that those of you who had expected me to deliver a technical, monographic paper tonight will understand why I have decided to ignore and neglect much that is important in order to try to achieve a summary, overall view of the man and his contributions to our national traditions.

1. Wilson and the Tradition of Morality in Politics and Policies

It is impossible to think of Woodrow Wilson without thinking of a somewhat stern moralist in politics. This image varies all the way from John Maynard Keynes's cruel caricature of Wilson as a narrow Puritan divine in his *The Economic Consequences of the Peace* to John Morton Blum's more friendly portrait in his *Woodrow Wilson and the Politics of Morality.* Underneath the stern image and behind the facade constructed by noble prose, there was a man intensely human, warm, responsive, and compassionate, well aware of his weaknesses. But the distortion of the Wilsonian image that has occurred has been mere distortion. The image itself is basically an accurate one. Woodrow Wilson was, first and foremost, a moralist who almost invariably viewed issues and behavior in terms of right and wrong. Indeed, his method in deciding upon any important matter was, first, to try to see the fundamental principles involved, and, next, to build policy upon the foundation that they provided.

It would have been remarkable had Wilson been constituted otherwise. He came from a long line of Presbyterian ministers on his mother's side and was the son of a distinguished Presbyterian minister. He literally grew up in the bosom of the church, imbibing unconsciously its traditions and faith. His own Christian faith changed and grew in response to new insights and experiences. But he remained throughout his life what he had been as a boy of seventeen when he published his first articles in the Wilmington *North Carolina Presbyterian* – a devout Christian and faithful churchman, whose every important action and policy was informed and profoundly influenced by Christian faith.

But I must not yield to the temptation, so strong to the biographer, to focus on my subject. We are more concerned about Wilson's lasting contributions than about him as an individual. And so we have to ask ourselves, to what degree did Wilson both reflect and reinforce American traditions of morality in politics and policies?

Those traditions, it is important to point out, had been absolutely central and controlling in the experience of the American people before the Civil War, just as they had been central in the great long western experience to this time. Judaism and Christianity, with their moral precepts, had furnished the foundations of American laws and institutions, the standards by which men judged officials and public policies, and the point of reference to which most Americans could and did appeal when they disagreed. So it was when Wilson was a boy and young man. But his maturing coincided with the beginning of new onslaughts against the historic Judeo-Christian cosmology and its affirmations about political life. These onslaughts came in the latter part of the nineteenth century, in the form of a new world view – scientific materialism – and new ethical systems derived from it – positivism, pragmatism, and relativism. Indeed, at the very moment that Wilson entered politics, a large body of American so-called intellectuals were hard at work trying to construct a scientific morality divorced from religion. This was the "new radicalism" of which the historian Christopher Lasch has recently written.

It is well known how Wilson, in company with other moralists in the main American tradition, like Theodore Roosevelt and William Jennings Bryan, left a deep impression of moral purpose on his era. Wilson was not merely a moralist, but a Christian moralist who believed deeply in moral law and the certainty of divine judgment when men and nations transgress that law; who tended to judge all measures on a basis of right and wrong; and who thought that right leadership, in the final analysis, consisted of helping people to find the paths of national righteousness. He was also an eloquent and moving moralist who, in political discourse, tended to raise every issue and conflict to a high stage upon which the human drama was being played out. Were the citizens of Trenton about to vote upon the adoption of commission government? Then they were being given an opportunity to prove that Americans were capable of enlightened self-government. Were the American people about to enter a terrible world war? Then they were being privileged to give their blood and treasure to extend the dominion of righteousness throughout the earth!

All scholars, of whatever persuasion they themselves happen to be, agree that the American people were united in their political strivings during the progressive era by common dedication to moral purpose, that it was this fact that really gave meaning to the period. For better or worse, much of the credit for perpetuating and strengthening the American tradition that all political questions are ultimately moral questions must go to Woodrow Wilson. He succeeded so well because he was himself deeply immersed in American traditions and history. As he put it in his Annual Message to Congress in 1914, "I have tried to know what America is, what her people think, what they are, what they most cherish and hold dear. I hope that some of their finer passions are in my own heart." He succeeded also because as an orator and writer, he was a sensitive poet who had not only absorbed great American political traditions but was also able to translate them into words so lofty and inspiring that they literally helped to change the course of human history.

I must add a postscript to this section lest I leave you with the impression, which is all too deeply imbedded in the popular view, that Wilson was a moralizer as well as a moralist, and one who always viewed issues rigidly in terms of simple black and white, right and wrong. That reminds me of the story to the effect that Wilson and onw of his colleagues at Princeton once fell into a very heated argument. Wilson's friend, hoping to end the discussion, said, "Well, Dr. Wilson, there are always two sides to every question." Whereupon Wilson is said to have shot back, "Yes, a right side and a wrong side!"

In actual fact, Wilson had a very sophisticated understanding of the sources and structure of Christian ethics. He had a powerful ego and drive toward dominance. He had a tendency to identify his own solutions with the moral law. He often sounded like a rigid moralizer. But the record reveals a man who well knew that morality, *per se,* does not suffice as a guide through the paradoxes and dilemmas of private and public life, one who could be enormously flexible about methods and details so long as they did not violate what he thought was right. I would suggest that Wilson, far from being the dogmatic, inflexible moralizer that he is often said to have been, was in fact a precursor of the modern American school of contextual ethics so well exemplified in our own time by the writings of Reinhold Niebuhr and Paul Lehmann. It is true, then what he had to say might have deeper meaning to our own generation than to his own.

2. *Wilson and the Tradition of Presidential Leadership*

Historians a century or two hence may well rate Wilson's contributions to the development of the presidential office as his most lasting contribution to the American political system. He had, almost from the moment that he began to think about political matters, a passion for orderly representative government, for doing political business in a proper manner. There is a story that his first constitution was one that he drafted while a boy in Augusta, Georgia, for a baseball association called the "Lightfoot Club." This may be mythological. The first Wilsonian written constitution that has survived is one that Wilson drafted in the summer of 1874 for an imaginative "Royal United Kingdom Yacht Club." Then followed constitutions for the Liberal Debating Club at Princeton in 1877, the Jefferson Literary Society at the University of Virginia in 1880, the Georgia House of Commons in 1882, the Hopkins House of Commons in 1884, the Wesleyan House of Commons in 1889, and so on down through the Covenant of the League of Nations in 1919.

Wilson had an equally strong passion for effective leadership and was forever trying to devise new machinery to facilitate leadership in American democratic government. His first solution was adoption of the British Cabinet form of government by the transformation of our Cabinet from an administrative body responsible to the President into a body responsible to Congress for leadership in legislative policies. He proposed this plan in the first article that he published in a national magazine — "Cabinet Government in the United States" (1879). He expanded this article into a book-length essay in 1882 called "Government by Debate." We will publish it for the first time in the second volume of the Wilson Papers. And he refined his argument in his most famous book, *Congressional Government,* published in 1885.

Wilson, actually, never abandoned his belief that the parliamentary system provided the best vehicle for responsible leadership in a democracy. We find him writing just before he was inaugurated in 1913 that sooner or later the President "must be made answerable to opinion in a somewhat more informal and intimate fashion — answerable, it may be, to the Houses whom he seeks to lead, either personally or through a Cabinet, as well as to the people for whom they speak." His plan to resign in order to permit his Republican opponent in 1916, Charles Evans Hughes, to assume the presidency immediately after the election, should Hughes win; Wilson's ill-fated appeal for the election of a Democratic Congress in 1918; and his unsuccessful attempt to make the election of 1920 a "solemn referendum" on the League of Nations were all later examples of Wilson's efforts to adapt the parliamentary system to American practice.

Ironically, Wilson, more than any other modern President, made it inevitable that the United States would retain the presidential system. He did this by his own success in showing for the first time, at least since Washington and Jefferson, what vast potentialities for leadership lie in the presidential office. Wilson's own views on this matter changed radically over the years. In *Congressional Government* he had dismissed the presidency as a useless fifth wheel in our constitutional system. But America's emergence to obvious world power in 1898, and Theodore Roosevelt's success in reviving the presidency as a vehicle of popular leadership, both brought new insights. And Wilson, in the last book that he ever wrote, *Constitutional Government in the United States* (1908), now saw the President in a new light — as potentially a powerful party leader and national spokesman who could, in fact, be the irresistible national leader if he but rightly interpreted the national will.

We take it for granted today that the President should give moral leadership to the nation; be the leader of his party; initiate legislation and see it through to passage; represent the people in all relations abroad; and of course administer the vast machinery of the federal government.

Earlier Presidents had excelled in one or more of these functions, but it was Wilson who first excelled in all of them. His first technique of leadership was to assert the position of spokesman of the people and to use public opinion as a spur on Congress. This he did by speeches and frequent informal statements and appeals in the press, by which he maintained intimate communication with the people. His second technique was to assert and maintain an irresistible leadership of his party in Congress. He did this in part through sheer force of personality, because he was determined to be a strong leader; in part through judicious use of the patronage and other instruments of political persuasion. His third technique was always to stay ahead of Congress in matters of legislative policy. That is, he read public opinion with a keen and sensitive eye, took the initiative in devising programs that the people demanded, and kept such heavy pressure on Capitol Hill that Congress could never catch its breath or act independently. His fourth technique was to take personal control of the conduct of foreign policy and, more important, to stand as the great national public spokesman of the American people in their foreign relations.

Whatever the means were that he used, Wilson more than any other President in our history fused the vast powers of the executive and legislative branches in his own person. He proved beyond cavil that the presidential office has sufficient inherent power to meet the needs of a great people and cope with the problems of the modern world.

3. Wilson and the Tradition of Government in the Service of the People

It has been the great political strength of the American people that they have always refused to be ideological or doctrinaire. Our religious and moral traditions have, to be sure, set very clear boundaries for political action. But within these boundaries, Americans have usually been able to meet problems as they arose by responding pragmatically and imaginatively in particular circumstances. Americans cherished state rights and local government, but love of state and locality did not prevent them from admitting that the Articles of Confederation was an impossible frame of national government. Americans have always valued liberty, including the liberty of every man to accumulate and enjoy property of his own. But, except for brief periods, they have never made a fetish of private property. Americans have always been suspicious of too much national government. But they have never translated this suspicion into an ideology. Even during the hey-day of laissez-faire doctrines in the nineteenth century, Americans had no compunctions against using federal power to preserve economic opportunity through liberal land policies and antitrust laws or, to cite another example, to abolish slavery and extend civil rights to freedmen.

Now it happened that Woodrow Wilson came to the presidency at a particularly crucial time in our domestic history. The American people had been convulsed for a generation, first by the agrarian revolt of the 1890's, then by what historians call the progressive movement. Industrialization and urbanization, with all their economic and social problems, had outstripped the progress of political institutions and legislation. There was a widespread discontent caused by the feeling that the old promise of an abundant and happy life for all Americans was being denied by great aggregations of private economic power and ruthless exploitation of resources and people. Discontent and a yearning for reform had disrupted parties since 1892 and had found a national voice in Theodore Roosevelt. Roosevelt, in fact, had taken the lead in the reconstruction of national policies by carrying through a great conservation effort and instituting an effective antitrust program on his own, and by persuading Congress to institute the first experiment in national regulation of private enterprise, that of the railroads.

Still, the great work in laying the foundations of a national political economy remained to be done when Wilson was inaugurated in 1913. And the fundamental decisions were yet to be made. Looking back, we can see that the American people had three choices in these years of upheaval, solutions that were then being warmly advocated by their particular devotees. First, they could have followed the advice of their conservative statesmen and some businessmen and continued severely to limit the exercise of federal power in economic life — they could have, for example, continued to permit private bankers to control the money supply and interest rates — in the expectation that so-called natural economic laws would themselves operate to maintain a free and abundant economy. Second, they could have gone down the path marked out by other ideologues — the Socialists — who advocated governmental ownership and operation of all major resources and productive facilities. Third, they had the choice of a middle road, neither laissez-faire nor socialistic, of seeking to preserve private ownership, initiative, and decision while at the same time attempting through regulation to reserve basic economic and social decisions to the people.

It was perhaps inevitable that Americans, given their history and traditions, should have chosen the third course. But it was not inevitable that the foundations of a new national economic policy would be well laid, or that particular solutions would be viable. It was Wilson's great contribution that, ignoring the maledictions of certain spokesmen of what we now call the right and the taunts of radicals on the left, he led Congress to devise the only kind of comprehensive national economic program that would satisfy the American people in the long run. It included a new banking monetary system and a new credit system for farmers, a new tariff policy, a program actively to protect competition, encouragement and (during the war) outright support of organized labor, a tax policy aimed at moderate redistribution of wealth, federal support of education, and federal control of child labor. Its sole objective was to make the American system of private enterprise work in the interests of all the people and not just a privileged few.

It is not the historian's task to say whether the outcome was good or bad. It is enough for him to note that the political economy in which *we* live, one marked by a considerable mixture of competition, private decision, and governmental participation and regulation, is the political economy first constructed in its basic features by Woodrow Wilson and the men, in and out of Congress, who labored with him.

4. *Wilson and the Tradition of Idealism in Foreign Policy*

Wilson went from one triumph to another in domestic affairs, at least until midway in his second term, when external events and circumstances began to generate a political backlash at home. But he had the satisfaction of knowing before he died that his contributions to the reconstruction of national economic policies would substantially survive. He may well have known that they would also provide the point of departure for future additions to the superstructure of the political economy. No such pattern of almost unbroken success marked his record as a maker of foreign policy. Indeed, the objective historian has to say that Wilson's record in foreign policy was, on the face of it a record largely of failure. Almost all of the objectives nearest to his heart, he failed to achieve. During the first two and a half years of the First World War he ardently desired to restore peace through his own mediation. He tried and failed. He sincerely, deeply, hoped to keep his country from being sucked into the war's vortex. He tried and failed. He worked with unbelievable energy to construct a just and lasting peace settlement after the war. He did not succeed fully. He destroyed his health in a supreme effort to persuade the Senate to consent to American membership in his creation, the League of Nations, and the American people to take leadership in rebuilding the shattered international community. Again, finally he failed. All this is not to suggest that Wilson's role in the international developments of his time was not a crucial one. There has never been much doubt about the significance of the part that he played. As Sir Winston Churchill once put it, while writing about the era of the First World War: "Writing with every sense of respect, it seems no exaggeration to pronounce that the action of the United States with its repercussions on the history of the world depended, during the awful period of Armageddon, upon the workings of this man's mind and spirit to the exclusion of almost every other factor; and that he played a part in the fate of nations incomparably more direct and personal than any other man."

And yet we and the world honor Wilson most for these apparent failures. We remember the heroic, often lonely, figure standing foursquare at Paris against forces of hatred, greed, and imperialism. We remember the dauntless fighter stumping the country in an incredible and nearly fatal forensic effort. We remember the man broken in health but not in spirit, unyielding to what he thought was shameful compromise, confident that the sovereign Lord of History would turn all events into their appointed channels. I am tempted to spend the balance of my time in further exposition of this stirring story. But an even more important subject demands our attention. That subject is the legacy that Wilson left to guide us in foreign policy.

That legacy is all the more relevant to our own time because Wilson happened to be President at a watershed in the history of American foreign policy and, more important, also almost perfectly embodied the conflicting American traditions in foreign policy. Like most other Americans of his day, Woodrow Wilson had little interest in European or Asiatic affairs when he came to the presidency. Like most of his fellow countrymen, he was at first an isolationist and something of a chauvinist, generally oblivious to the great forces that were catapulting the United States against its will into a decisive role in international affairs. Ironically, he lost his leadership and ceased to speak for the preponderant majority once he repudiated the traditions of isolationism and chauvinism and embraced the still young tradition begun by Theodore Roosevelt of a great power actively at work in the affairs of the world to promote security and peace. But let us look at some of Wilson's contributions to American traditions in foreign policy.

First, there is the tradition that Theodore Roosevelt had begun only imperfectly and Wilson brought to its first culmination, the tradition of disinterested helpfulness to nations struggling toward self-government and a more abundant economic life. Cynics will smile and say that no great power can ever be altruistic in dealing with other nations, particularly small and helpless nations. They are of course right to some degree. But it *is* a matter of degree, and Woodrow Wilson, more than any other statesman of the modern era, unless it be Gladstone, sincerely believed that America existed in order to vindicate moral principles, provide an example to the world, and work for the welfare and happiness of men everywhere. He believed that foreign policy should not only *not* be used for material ends, but also that it should not even be defined into terms of material interests. America's mission in the world was to fulfill God's plan by unselfish service to mankind. He tried to implement such a policy in the four corners of the earth. Sometimes he failed, or only partially succeeded, as in the Dominican Republic and Haiti. Sometimes he succeeded, as in Mexico, where he played a large role in the success of the Mexican Revolution, or as in Europe, where, during the War and Peace Conference, he proclaimed and vindicated American altruism. But the point is that he established the tradition so firmly that it would revive again, once Americans were faced with new challenges during and after the Second World War.

Second, there is the tradition that all peoples have the right, qualified only by their capacity to exercise it responsibly and without doing injury to others, to self-determination and self-government. It goes without saying that this is the oldest American tradition in foreign policy, but Wilson revived it and made it the cardinal American tradition of our own day. And by his eloquence and efforts, he helped to destroy old empires and spelled the end to colonialism and old-fashioned imperialism.

Third, there is the tradition of the peaceful settlement of international disputes and the avoidance of war if conceivably possible. This tradition, as the fundamental basis of American foreign policy, is much more recent in our history than most of us realize. Americans went to war three times during the nineteenth century to settle international disputes, and our more candid historians have been frank to admit that there was very dubious moral justification for belligerency on at least two of those occasions. Wilson was of course not alone in implanting the tradition of peaceful settlement of disputes, but he played the largest role by his word and example. Twice he personally prevented seemingly irresistible events from plunging the United States into war with Mexico. He fought desperately to avoid participation in the World War, enduring egregious violations of American neutral rights and taunts by his enemies that he was a moral coward, afraid, rather than too proud, to fight. He accepted belligerency when he saw no alternative, but he took careful pains to write into fundamental international law the principle that all international disputes, whether large or small, had to be settled by arbitration or conciliation.

Fourth, there is the tradition, also controlling in our own time, of the American people committing their resources and power to the quest for peace through international cooperation. It is almost trite to say that Wilson, by his fight for American membership in and leadership of the League of Nations, did more than any other single man to build this tradition. The fact that he failed momentarily is of minor significance in the long run. The important fact is that he was the man who spoke the word of truth to a future if not to his own generation. He was the prophet, teacher, and builder. He was the true realist of his time. His words and voice and vision never died. Even in defeat he taught, inspired, and challenged a generation of young men who, as leaders of the United States in the following generation, would remember his precepts and example.

Perhaps it was as teacher that Wilson made his most lasting contribution to American traditions. For traditions are carried on by men, not by impersonal historical forces, and young men usually have to learn from older men before they can carry standards themselves. What a training school in leadership and statesmanship it was that Woodrow Wilson conducted! Out of it came Herbert Hoover, Norman Thomas, Bernard Baruch, Newton D. Baker, Franklin Roosevelt, Cordell Hull, John Foster Dulles, Allen Dulles, Dwight D. Eisenhower, and a host of other Americans who would in their own day make their own contributions to American traditions. For this and other contributions, we honor Woodrow Wilson as a maker and molder of our past, present, and future, for with him the sword, when it flashed, carried the light of heaven upon its blade.

FRANKLIN D. ROOSEVELT: THE QUEST FOR SECURITY

By Frank Freidel

Franklin D. Roosevelt's noblest dreams were in the realm of security. He aspired to a nation and a world without want and without war. Yet it was over these aspirations that the angriest controversies raged during his Presidency and for years after his death. In spite of these controversies, Roosevelt's objectives came to be accepted as responsibilities by each of his successors as President. Roosevelt sought to enlist the full energies of the Federal government in the fostering of the economic welfare not only of the American people, but as far as possible, of all peoples. He undertook responsibility for the collective security of the American people and of other peoples of the world, threatened by aggressor nations. Put in another way, it can be said that Roosevelt sought a more abundant, more secure way of life for the American people and for all humanity.

The years Roosevelt dominated were a time of extreme insecurity – the age of the great depression and the global war. It was a time of tragedy in which he provided positive leadership as the spokesman for a better America and a better world. Although a quarter of a century has now elapsed, yet this era is still of vital significance to us in 1967.

For a dozen years, beginning in 1933, the President, with his jaunty optimism, his warm friendliness, and his flare for the dramatic, dominated the newspaper front pages, the radios, and the newsreels of the nation. He was a controversial figure, fervently loved by his friends and supporters, and equally hated by his enemies, who charged he was reducing the nation to fascism, socialism, and bankruptcy. All these sins can be summed up in a phrase: Roosevelt by becoming the champion of the under-privileged was threatening the old established order of things.

The outbreak of war in Europe in 1939 moved the debate over Roosevelt into the realm of foreign policy. As Hitler's *panzer* divisions swept to the Channel and threatened to invade England, Roosevelt appeared to some Americans as a war-monger who wished needlessly to embroil the nation in conflict; and to others he appeared to be the one man who could save Western civilization.

After his death, controversy continued between those who regarded him as having been foolish in his war strategy and a dupe of the Russians, and those who hailed his vision in heading a coalition of triumphant allies and in building a new world order to be based on collective security. There was no expectation that collective security would in time entail heavy military preparedness and the fighting of endless limited war on far-off battlefronts. Roosevelt was mourned as a hero at the time of his funeral, but during the years of frightening cold war that unexpectedly followed, his reputation seriously suffered. More recently, as the Roosevelt years have receded in time, he has ceased to be a focal point of political controversy and his repute has been once more on the rise.

It is now amply clear that Roosevelt contributed greatly toward furthering the age-old goals of the American people, and indeed of mankind. He aspired to a better way of life not only for those of his own country but for those of all nations. He was a man of vision, and we honor him for his vision.

A President without vision would be no leader at all. A President with vision, but lacking the political skill to implement it, would be almost as sorry a leader. Roosevelt happily combined vision with political virtuosity. Often he was cautious in method, partly because as a skilled political leader he was ready to undertake only what at the moment seemed within the realm of possibility, and partly because as a truly religious man, whose humanitarianism was transcendent, he would never sanction means that were not in keeping with the idealistic ends toward which he was striving. His caution occasionally caused even those to whom he was nearest and dearest to become annoyed, for his thinking was based solidly in the values of the nineteenth century in which he was brought up. His wife, Eleanor Roosevelt, less ready to make allowances for political obstacles, must at times have become a bit impatient with him. Once during the second World War she went with her husband to see off Prime Minister Churchill, who had been visiting them. As they waved to the departing guest, the President remarked to her that he felt that Churchill, whom he held in deep affection, was hopelessly Victorian. "You too, Franklin," Mrs. Roosevelt thought to herself, "are much in the nineteenth century."

And, in some respects, so President Roosevelt was, but in a rather salutary way. On January 30, 1882 — eighty-five years ago — Franklin Delano Roosevelt was born into a well-to-do family on an estate at Hyde Park, New York. It was a family of a sort rare in the United States, possessing modest wealth and high social position for several generations. Its members, thanks to their social status, not only enjoyed self-assurance, but also felt a keen responsibility to improve the lot of the less fortunate. Roosevelt's mother impressed upon her son that from those to whom so much is given, much is expected. His education was patrician, but both at Groton School and Harvard University his masters and professors urged him to shoulder responsibilities toward society. Thus in the comfortable, stable years of the end of the nineteenth century, this young man, growing up in what seemed to those as well-to-do as he to be a secure and settled society, learned to hold himself to high standards of religion, ethics, and social service – all in a rather paternalistic sort of way. The spirit with which he was indoctrinated was that of *noblesse oblige;* in English terms, the spirit of the Tory radicalism of Disraeli. This was the Victorian root of his thinking, which, unlike the ideology of many of his classmates, he was to transcend in the twentieth century.

But some of the Victorianism never wore off. In his first term in the New York legislature, Roosevelt considered himself a Grover Cleveland Democrat, dedicated above all to clean government; and in some respects he functioned like one. As President he retained a bit of the Cleveland viewpoint, having at heart a horror of Federal deficits, which led him drastically to cut spending in 1937, even while old-line Cleveland Democrats like Senator Carter Glass of Virginia were excoriating him for his fiscal apostasy. In the case of Roosevelt the apostacy predominated, and perhaps this too, in part, was traceable to his Victorian upbringing. It might be argued that he had been reared in so secure and self-assured a fashion that, like the Victorian Tories of England, he could dare to be radical.

When Roosevelt came of age in the early years of the twentieth century, new winds of change were already blowing briskly, as many young middle-class Americans became outraged at the social injustices they saw around them and sought vigorously through political means to bring about a better social order. Eleanor Roosevelt, even as a very young woman, was involved in this movement, working with unfortunates in the slums of New York City. After she and Franklin Roosevelt became engaged, she showed her handsome young fiance conditions he had not known existed. In these same years, her uncle, President Theodore Roosevelt (who was Franklin Roosevelt's distant cousin) strongly influenced the young man toward political participation in what came to be known as the Progressive movement. This movement still bore a considerable mark of paternalism but was moving toward reform of social and economic inequalities through modifications in the laws rather than through mere dependence upon private philanthropy.

So it was that in 1910, Franklin D. Roosevelt, whose work as a law clerk had become a bore to him, decided to enter politics. Since his branch of the family had been traditionally Democratic and since the opportunity to run for the New York State Senate came from the Democratic Party, he entered politics as a Democrat rather than as a Republican like Theodore Roosevelt. But Progressivism was a vital force within both major parties and Franklin Roosevelt demonstrated in the New York State Senate that while he still gave obeisance to the principles of Grover Cleveland, more than that he was an exuberant young Progressive. When a great Progressive Democrat, Woodrow Wilson, was elected President, Roosevelt went to Washington in 1913 to serve as Assistant Secretary of the Navy. In his seven years' service as a junior administrator in the New Freedom he came to accept unreservedly the Wilsonian ideals in domestic reform and foreign policy.

Both Theodore Roosevelt and Woodrow Wilson and their two versions of Progressivism – the New Nationalism and the New Freedom – indelibly impressed Franklin D. Roosevelt. I suspect that he was far more impressed by the dynamic leadership of these men than by the specifics of their programs. Frances Perkins, who served as Secretary of Labor during the New Deal, remembers young Franklin

Roosevelt, when she first met him at a party, talking to her with the warmest enthusiasm about Theodore Roosevelt, but without more than the fuzziest notion of T.R.'s policies. His admiration for Wilson was matched by a similar haziness about the economics of the New Freedom. Conservation and naval policy were exceptions; in these areas young Roosevelt was already expert. And already before the First World War he was interested in city and regional planning.

As President, Franklin D. Roosevelt appreciated T.R.'s economic policies, but it was the first Roosevelt's personal dynamism that he especially tried to follow. When he was a beginner in politics, F.D.R. used to entertain his audiences by describing how he, as a little boy, and his father had been ushered into President Cleveland's presence and the sad, weary Cleveland had intoned, "My boy, I hope when you grow up you'll never have the misfortune to become President," and contrasting this with an episode at the White House in the T.R. years when one of a group of young people gathered around T.R. asked him how he liked being President and T.R. replied, "Bully; simply bully!" No one ever doubted during F.D.R.'s years in the White House which view he took of the Presidency. In keeping with his own personality and partly through the example of his wife's Uncle Ted, Franklin D. Roosevelt brought a similar restless dynamism to the Presidency. He also loved excitement and action. He too was temperamentally unsuited to serve as the custodian of the status quo. In each of these men there was a curious interplay between his conservative grounding and his quest for new experiences for himself and the nation. Woodrow Wilson's influence upon F.D.R. was of a different sort, that of a rather austere moral preceptor.

So it was that in inclination if not in firm economic views Franklin D. Roosevelt carried much of the spirit of

Progressivism to the White House. In some respects he never ceased to be the panting youngster trailing at the heels of T.R. and the awe-struck schoolboy absorbing moral lessons from Wilson. As President he filled the roles of both predecessors, leading the American people in ever-exciting chase, but pausing now and then to deliver to them an eloquent homily. What Roosevelt had also learned from these two great Progressives was the art of being President. He demonstrated by some remarks he made in 1936 how shrewdly he had observed his teachers: "Theodore Roosevelt lacked Woodrow Wilson's appeal to the fundamental and failed to stir, as Wilson did, the truly profound moral and social convictions. Wilson, on the other hand, failed where Theodore Roosevelt succeeded in stirring people to enthusiasm over specific individual events, even though these specific events may have been superficial in comparison with the fundamentals."

In his Progressive baggage Franklin D. Roosevelt carried an extraordinary grasp of political strategy and tactics and a preoccupation with the humane and the moral, rather than the economic, aspect of issues.

Only twelve years intervened between Roosevelt's apprenticeship in the Wilson administration and his inauguration as President. During the first World War he achieved a reputation as a dynamic young administrator who could "get things done." He became an enthusiast for the war agencies as a means of accomplishing economic miracles. In 1920, when he was only 38 years old, he was nominated for the Vice Presidency on the Democratic ticket and for several months campaigned with energy and dedication on behalf of the Democratic Party and President Wilson's dream of American participation in the League of Nations.

But 1920 turned out to be a black year for Roosevelt, and the one that followed was still blacker. Americans in

1920 were sick of war and tired of Wilsonian idealism; the Democrats were badly defeated at the polls. The following summer, Roosevelt, aged 39, was stricken with poliomyletis (infantile paralysis) in a form so severe that he nearly died. After months of acute suffering he recovered his health, but his legs were useless. Refusing to leave politics, as well as to give up hope that somehow he would reacquire the capacity to walk, he set forth with dauntless courage and unquenchable good humor and optimism to recoup his personal disaster. In the struggle he had behind him the strength and intelligence of Mrs. Roosevelt who, previously a painfully shy woman, threw herself into Democratic politics in order to represent her husband and serve as his eyes and ears. Roosevelt never again was able to walk unassisted, although in time, through the aid of metal braces, he succeeded in giving in public the appearance of walking, of being only lame instead of (as was the reality) paraplegic; whose ordinary behind-the-scenes method of locomotion was a wheel-chair.

In politics Roosevelt's comeback was startlingly triumphant. In the election year, 1928, which nationally marked another Republican landslide, he was elected Governor of New York. By 1932, when he was elected President, the United States was deep in the trough of the worst economic depression in its history, a depression which was wracking the entire world. To the present generation, the only generation in American history which has grown to maturity without living through a painful economic downturn, the severity and suffering of the early 1930's must seem almost unbelievable. Between one-quarter and one-third of the working force was unemployed, one-quarter of the farmers had lost their land, and most Americans to some degree were feeling the economic pinch Relief funds to sustain those completely destitute were becoming exhausted, and payments to those who did receive aid averaged only fifty cents per family per day. Midwest farmers kept themselves warm by burning corn, while the hungry of the nation's cities hunted for food scraps on the garbage dumps. Edmund Wilson described one desperate Chicago woman who took off her glasses before scavenging so that she would not see the maggots and half-spoiled meat. Bank runs in February, 1933 had forced state governors to proclaim banking holidays; almost every bank in the United States was closed when Roosevelt delivered his inaugural address.

Many Americans were asking themselves if democracy could survive this depression ordeal. Italy and Germany were already travelling along totalitarian routes toward attempted recovery, the paths of Fascism and Nazism; and German and Italian editors, under the tutelage of Hitler and Mussolini, were predicting that the United States would be forced to follow a similar course. Radicals throughout the world saw socialism or communism as the only way out. Anxious observers in many nations watched to see what direction the New Deal would take. The answer came when Roosevelt took his oath of office as President on March 4, 1933. He spoke with sternness and confidence as he sought to stem the national panic; and with anger and moral fervor be blamed the depression upon those American business leaders who had mismanaged the economy in the 1920's, and held the bankers themselves largely responsible for the nation's plight. While sitting in his pew at St. James Church in Hyde Park, New York, the Sunday before he took office, he had thought of lines for his inaugural address that set a major theme of his administration:

"The money changers have fled from their high seats in the temple of our civilization. We may now restore that temple to the ancient truths. The measure of the restoration lies in the extent to which we apply social values more noble than mere monetary profit."

It is well to note these words and more words like them in Roosevelt's first inaugural. Their call to a moral crusade was from the outset as integral a part of Roosevelt's New Deal as his better-remembered promise of immediate, massive efforts to achieve recovery and his famous admonition, "We have nothing to fear but fear itself."

Recovery was urgently first on Roosevelt's calendar. First it was essential to re-open the banks, and through a most conservative piece of legislation this was done. Hoarders returned their cash and the crisis was over. Congress at the moment had tremendous pressure upon it — Roosevelt was so enormously popular — so Roosevelt kept it in session and in the famous first One Hundred Days rushed through it the wide panoply that comprised the first phase of the New Deal. One rather awe-stricken Republican congressman from Maine wrote candidly to a friend two weeks after Roosevelt took office, "There can be no doubt that at the moment the President has an extraordinary support throughout the country and is able to do with the Congress as he wills. I suppose prudence dictates that one should not attempt to swim against the tide."

First there were emergency laws, intended to bring about speedy recovery and to provide immediate relief to the millions of people who were in acute want. That this economic legislation went in contrary directions did not bother Roosevelt in the least. Like the Cleveland Democrats in trying to be fiscally conservative, he economized drastically in the routine functions of the government; and like the Progressives (who also favored the cuts) he eliminated the favors the Federal government had been extending to business. The statistical services of the Census Bureau and the scientific services of the Bureau of Standards were not fully restored until the late 1930's. Simultaneously, and again in keeping with the views of most progressives, he wanted to keep taxes up, and in 1935 insisted upon drastic increases in the higher income brackets. He was thus fulfilling in the early 1930's most of the demands of the economically orthodox, who insisted that the route to recovery must be marked by cuts in government spending, higher taxes, and a balanced budget.

Critics of the orthodox view were numerous and powerful in the early New Deal years. They insisted that orthodoxy could lead only to further depression at a time when one of the nation's most acute problems was the existing degree of deflation. The buying power of the dollar had increased so drastically — that is to say, the price of farm products and most consumer goods except for steel, autos, and durable goods had dropped so drastically — that it seemed unlikely that mortgages, bond issues, and other debts incurred in the boom times of the 1920's could ever be paid. Western agrarians like Senator Thomas of Oklahoma pressed for massive inflation to bring prices up; certain sophisticated and conservative Easterners favored a quite limited step, that of going off the gold standard. Roosevelt, to the horror of the orthodox, did take the nation off the gold standard. He tried to raise farm prices through the triple A and to increase prices and buying power through the N.R.A. Both of these agencies, like several others of the early New Deal, were modelled after emergency wartime agencies, but their task was just the reverse: to inhibit production rather than to increase it; to foster price increases rather than to inhibit them. Like the war agencies they had to function on what in practice was pretty much a voluntary basis. Federal enforcement was thinner than that of Prohibition. The patriotic incentives to cooperate after the passing of the first euphoria in the summer of 1933 were less than in wartime, and the economic or profit incentives still less. The AAA worked fairly well, thanks to a drought which cut seriously into production; the N.R.A. not as well.

So by the fall of 1933, Roosevelt had become less orthodox in his economic policies and tried to raise prices through manipulating the gold content of the dollar. And to the horror of his early conservative supporters, his humanitarianism was winning out over his insistence upon government economy. The sums he was spending upon relief, upon keeping people from starving, began to mount to a degree that in the 1930's seemed astronomical. It is not difficult to see why Roosevelt acted as he did in the economic realm. He was more a humanitarian, progressive moralist and skillful politician than he was a devotee of economic orthodoxy. What was more, he liked to experiment. An economic program working at cross purposes, simultaneously toward deflation and inflation, made perfectly good sense politically, since it rallied behind Roosevelt the great national consensus. No hobgoblins of inconsistency kept Roosevelt awake at night; indeed, eclecticism was second nature to him. There were among his advisers, as Raymond Moley, the chief Brain Truster, pointed out in a most illuminating essay in 1934, the gold inflationists who thought this step alone would suffice, the Bull Moose-type planners who favored positive government intervention in the economy, and the devotees of Brandeis, the heirs of the New Freedom, who wished the government to play a limited, rather negative role in preventing bigness and centralization. And as Moley pointed out, Roosevelt blandly mixed all three prescriptions in varying degrees. He simply did not think first and foremost in terms of economic doctrine. In the winter of 1932–33 when President Hoover was using the issue of war debts to try to pressure Roosevelt to avow complete orthodoxy (including an international gold standard), Roosevelt argued persuasively with one of his economic advisers, Rexford G. Tugwell, that the question of war debts was not really economic at all, but political. Much economic controversy throughout the New Deal years must have seemed to Roosevelt to be fundamentally political if one is to judge by the way he acted. Public pressure and concomitant (or differing) congressional pressure, together with his own evolving views, took him along a varying course between 1933 and 1939. As a master politician he kept behind him a substantial working majority in Congress: there were Southern Democrats, most of whom were basically conservative and who controlled key committees, but who were tied to him personally and by long-standing habits of party loyalty; there were the old-line urban Democrats of the North, again regulars, who were enormously pressured by their constituents to support the New Deal; there were the new Democrats in Congress from both South and North who were ardent New Dealers; and, finally, there were the Progressive Republicans, to which Roosevelt catered beyond their numerical strength, especially to a trio of senators: Johnson of California, La Follette of Wisconsin, and Norris of Nebraska. It may be possible that the urging he received from La Follette was a more important factor than the pressure from Huey Long in leading Roosevelt to submit to Congress the 1935 bill that hostile newspapers labelled the "soak the rich" tax program. It is also possible that Roosevelt may have been seeking to forestall more drastic Progressive action when he initiated a virgorous anti-trust program under Thurman Arnold late in the New Deal. In any event, whatever Roosevelt's maneuvers may have lacked in economic consistency they made good sense politically. In effect he was a clever chef preparing a fairly wide variety of ideological dishes, some of which would appeal to almost any customer. Of course, those whom the President labelled the "economic royalists" to the right, or the "lunatic fringe" to the left, would accept nothing the President proposed. They wanted either intact retention of an old order or its utter destruction. Roosevelt and the vast majority of Americans whether in the Democratic or Republican parties rejected outright both alternatives. They wished to improve the existing system. Amid the ideological debates of the mid-1930's the notable poet Archibald MacLeish, a New Dealer, brilliantly stated Roosevelt's motivation and the American response to it:

"Let no man miss the point of Mr. Roosevelt's hold upon the minds of the citizens of this republic. Men's minds are fired by Mr. Roosevelt because they are sick to nausea of the rich bankers and their economists upon the one side and the great revolutionaries and their economists upon the other, repeating over and over that the world is ruled by incontrovertible economic laws which it is not only blasphemy but idiocy to oppose, and which lead inevitably to certain fixed and inescapable conclusions. . . . It is only to the free, inventive gestures of the human soul that men wholly and believingly respond. They will, in a crisis, rise against arrogance. They may, for a time, fight from hatred. But only to hope will they give themselves entirely."

Roosevelt, disdaining the dogmas of both Reaction and Revolution, but listening with unusual receptivity to innumerable proposals for improving the existing order, proceeded along his experimental way. It was pragmatism in action, but he never dignified his course with such high-flown language, frankly referring to it as a trial-and-error method. This was the classic pattern of operation of nineteenth-century American inventors; and Roosevelt, who had earlier made New York an experimental laboratory, deliberately carried this technique to Washington. What is most important, it worked, although not entirely in keeping with the preconceptions of Roosevelt and his Brain Trust. The great projects in the area of regional planning and conservation (TVA, CCC, the planting of shelter belts on the Great Plains, and the like), all of which were of keen interest to Roosevelt, did indeed succeed much as planned. They demonstrated that Federal planning and development on a regional scale could work and that an enormous production of electric power could stimulate small enterprise and raise living standards. On the other hand, planned communities like Arthurdale, West Virginia, so dear to the heart of Mrs. Roosevelt, were abysmal failures and were abandoned. And out of a great recovery scheme like the NRA came not the rationalized upturn of industry that had been envisaged, but a Federal guarantee of the right of employees to bargain collectively with an employer, the establishment of Federal standards of wages and hours, and the prohibition of child labor. Roosevelt envisaged the Social Security Act as not only a humane measure to aid the aged, the orphaned, and the unemployed, but also as an economic device to create what a later generation has labelled the "built-in stabilizers" of the economy. On the other hand, Roosevelt at first had opposed as impractical another successful stabilizer, Federal Deposit Insurance; and as I earlier suggested, he had not thought at all in terms of what eventually became the basic New Deal solution to deflation and depression, namely, massive government spending. He had insisted upon a quite slow and careful spending of the huge public works appropriation which was integral part of the National Industrial Recovery Act, even though he counted upon this money to stimulate the construction and allied industries. The heavy spending during the first four years of the New Deal was almost inadvertent on his part and came about because Harry Hopkins, the head of the Federal relief programs, worked more effectively on his humanitarian spirit than did Secretary of the Treasury Henry Morgenthau, Jr. upon his economic orthodoxy. And, finally, it was Congress, pressured by the American Legion and other veterans' organizations, that, over his veto, passed a measure to pay a bonus to veterans of the first World War. Since most of the recipients were relatively well off, the bonus money was spent for automobiles and refrigerators and the renovation of homes rather than on mere subsistence items and thereby markedly stimulated the economy. According to most economists, it was the relief and public works spending plus the veterans' bonus that started the wavering economy on the way to recovery in 1935 and 1936. By early 1937, most economic indices, with the vital exception of employment, were approaching 1929 levels. At this point, orthodoxy won out with Roosevelt. He cut government spending drastically, and the country plunged into a painful recession. Regretfully he asked Congress for large sums to resume government spending, and even before defense orders carried the nation into a war boom, a steady recovery had once more been achieved. It was in this trial-and-error fashion that Roosevelt and the nation's economists moved toward the fabrication of counter-cyclical enonomic policies for the government. This was not a Keynesian, so much as a peculiarly American, brand of economics, which in time developed far beyond Keynes's formulations.

Thus, Roosevelt and the Congress and daring administrators evolved a new relationship between the government and the economy which has remained the foundation of American economic policy ever since. It is this relationship, going far beyond either practice or theory in the Progressive era or the era of the first World War, which makes the New Deal such a significant watershed in American history. As one historian, Richard Hofstadter, has pointed out, it represented a positive intervention in the economy on behalf of the welfare of the American people, replacing the more negative role of the earlier decades. And as another historian, Arthur Schlesinger, Jr., has emphasized, it succeeded within the traditional democratic framework in bringing effective governmental intervention to the support of the general welfare. Roosevelt, whatever his political enemies might charge, never could countenance experimenting with totalitarian means to achieve humane ends. To him it was unthinkable to be other than democratic in political philosophy as well as in party affiliation.

Long before 1937 when Roosevelt was inaugurated for his second term as President, he had made it emphatically clear that he felt the government of the United States must assume responsibility for the improvement of the welfare of the American people. In his inaugural address that year, he dedicated his second administration to the elimination of poverty among the one-third of the American people that were "ill-housed, ill-clad, ill-nourished." He asserted:

"I see a United States which can demonstrate that, under democratic methods of government national wealth can be translated into a spreading volume of human comforts hitherto unknown, and the lowest standard of living can be raised far above the level of mere subsistence."

This was President Roosevelt's vision for the United States, and from it he never wavered.

In that age of totalitarianism and militarism, President Roosevelt faced the even more serious task of maintaining security from without. In his first years as President, Roosevelt felt that the United States, protected by a strong navy, should exert a moral force for peace throughout the world without itself risking involvement in foreign wars. He devoted himself to the rebuilding of the Navy, and by 1941 it was largely a new fleet that protected the United States.

Within the western hemisphere, Roosevelt successfully promoted the "Good Neighbor" policy, which to a striking degree was a fore-runner of the policies the United States has maintained toward all friendly nations in the years since 1945. As early as 1928 he publicly rejected the older relationships with Latin America as outmoded and unfair. By the beginning of 1933, Roosevelt later wrote in a remarkably revealing memorandum, he "began to visualize a wholly new attitude toward other American Republics based on an honest and sincere desire, first, to remove from their minds all fear of American aggression — territorial or financial — and, second, to take them into a kind of hemispheric partnership in which no Republic would obtain undue advantage." In his inaugural address in March, 1933, he pledged the nation to the policy of the "good neighbor," and before the end of the year began to spell out in detail what he meant.

Late in 1936, Roosevelt journeyed to Buenos Aires to address the Inter-American Conference meeting there. He and the fellow delegates were alarmed over the rise of Hitler and feared the spread of war to this hemisphere. He discussed means of joint action to preserve the peace, then looked ahead even further:

"In addition. . .we can strive even more strongly than in the past to prevent the creation of those conditions which give rise to war. Lack of social or political justice within the borders of any Nation is always cause for concern. Through democratic processes we can strive to achieve for the Americas the highest possible standard of living conditions for all our people. Men and women blessed with political freedom, willing to work and able to find work, rich enough to maintain their families and to educate their children, contented with their lot in life and on terms of friendship with their neighbors, will defend themselves to the utmost, but will never consent to take up arms for a war of conquest."

The raising of living standards was not enough in the 1930's, important though it was in long-range thinking. The aggressive actions of Hitler, whom Roosevelt had looked upon from the outset as a menace to world peace, together with Mussolini and the Japanese, gradually forced Roosevelt to become an advocate of collective security. Even so, he was far from consistent. In the fall of 1937, in response to new Japanese forays into China, he proposed, speaking in Chicago, that the peace-loving nations impose a quarantine against aggressors to contain the contagion of war. Apparently he had in mind nothing more than a joint breaking off of diplomatic relations but the speech created such a furor that he backtracked rapidly.

These were the years, between 1937 and 1941, in which to those favoring strong action, Roosevelt seemed to be hesitant and cautious while those fearing intervention assailed him as being foxy and deceitful. The so-called isolationists charged he was deliberately maneuvering the nation toward war. Yet beyond question Roosevelt did abhor war, and was speaking from his heart when he said in 1936, "I have seen war. . . . I hate war." He hoped fervently to keep Americans out of whatever war might develop. Even during the early months of the second World War before the fall of France, he hoped that the United States by supplying materiel of war to the foes of Hitler could contribute to the downfall of the Axis without direct involvement. Certain it is too, that by the fall of 1940 he regarded the victorious Axis as a menace to the United States and was by no means sure involvement could or should be avoided. Speaking in Boston that fall, he used words the isolationists subsequently mocked:

"I have said this before, but I shall say it again and again and again:

"Your boys are not going to be sent into any foreign wars."

Roosevelt was making the mental reservation which he did not explain to his audience, that an attack upon the United States and the resulting conflict would not constitute involvement in a foreign war. Through the succeeding year, although the Navy became increasingly active in convoying supplies to the Atlantic and in fighting Nazi submarines, Hitler did not declare war.

The attack came, rather, in the Pacific. Roosevelt had been pressing the Japanese hard to force them to abandon their aggressive course in Asia, making a serious miscalculation in thinking they would back down. When evidence came in the late fall of 1941 that the Japanese, rather, would attack, he and his advisors made a second miscalculation. They expected the attack to fall solely upon Singapore and the Dutch East Indies, and perhaps upon the Philippines. I cannot emphasize strongly enough that neither Roosevelt nor his advisers had any advance knowledge, or even suspicion, that the attack might be upon Hawaii. They were guilty of miscalculation, not chicanery.

The Japanese strike at Pearl Harbor brought national unity, and Roosevelt concentrated upon his roles as Commander-in-Chief of the armed forces and planner for the postwar future. Through compromises among the American chiefs of staff, and between the Americans and their allies, the British, he helped devise winning strategy. The Chief Historian of the Department of the Army, Kent Roberts Greenfield, in summing up Roosevelt's contribution, argued that from the beginning to the end he sought to utilize the United States as "the arsenal of Democracy," and by confronting the enemy with an overwhelming weight of armaments "to crush them with a minimum expenditure of American lives."

At Casablanca Conference in 1942, Roosevelt, with the approval of Churchill, suddenly propounded the formula of "unconditional surrender." It has been argued that this formula played into the hands of the diehard Nazis, but it may also be argued that it avoided confusion in setting peace terms, rallied the Allies, and made no real difference to the Nazis.

Even before the United States entered the war, Roosevelt had given much thought to the future. In addressing Congress in January, 1941 he enunciated the goal of the four basic freedoms — freedom of speech and worship and freedom from want and fear — for everyone everywhere. Less often noted than the Four Freedoms is the way President Roosevelt at the same time spelled out his interpretation of democracy not only for the United States, but by implication for other nations as well. He said:

"There is nothing mysterious about the foundations of a healthy and strong democracy. The basic things expected by our people of their political and economic systems are simple. They are equality of opportunity for youth and for others; jobs for those who can work; security for those who need it; the ending of special privileges for the few; the preservation of civil liberties for all; the enjoyment of the fruits of scientific progress in a wider and constantly rising standard of living.

"These are the simple and basic things that must never be lost sight of in the turmoil and unbelievable complexity of our modern world. The inner and abiding strength of our economic and political systems is dependent upon the degree to which they fulfill these expectations."

To Roosevelt these words were not merely fine-sounding generalizations, but a clear statement of the goals toward which he was determined to work. So, when on August 14, 1941, together with Prime Minister Churchill, Roosevelt initialled a press communique called the "Atlantic Charter," he took quite literally the third of its enumerated principles; that: "They respect the right of all peoples to choose the form of government under which they will live; and they wish to see sovereign rights and self-government restored to them." To Roosevelt these words applied not only to those peoples who were suffering Nazi occupation, but also those living under colonial governments. On his way to the Casablanca Conference at the beginning of 1943, he stopped at Bathurst, capital of the British colony, Gambia, on the coast of West Africa. He was appalled at what he saw there and thenceforth gave much thought to the gradual dismantling of colonial empires and the extension of economic and technical aid to former colonial peoples.

Relations with Russia throughout the war were of even more concern to Roosevelt. He devoted much effort to being concilliatory toward these suspicious allies, meeting many of their demands for Lend Lease goods. At Teheran and Yalta he did his best to establish friendly relations with Stalin and seemed, on his return from the Yalta Conference of 1945, to have driven good bargains. Almost immediately the Russians began to renege. Roosevelt had been too optimistic about Stalin and too ready to discount realistic reports from Moscow, yet his basic premise was scarcely debatable: that the future peace of the world depended upon workable relations between the United States and Russia. Roosevelt hoped that the two great powers would be able to resolve their differences and cooperate within a new international agency to keep the peace, the United Nations.

Late in the war, Roosevelt's health deteriorated rapidly; he appeared like a wraith in some of the pictures taken at Yalta. It was while he was trying to regain strength at Warm Springs, Georgia that he was stricken with a massive cerebral hemmorhage and died. The day before, he had been working on a Jefferson Day speech. "The only limit to our realization of tomorrow will be our doubts of today," read the final sentence of the typed draft. He added in his own hand, "Let us move forward with strong and active faith."

DWIGHT D. EISENHOWER – THE TRAINING AND THE TASKS

By Alfred D. Chandler, Jr.

It is indeed a great pleasure to be here not only as a speaker but as a member of your society. The reason I have joined the Michigan Society is that through conferences and correspondence with Russell Lucas, Past Governor of the Society, I became aware that there was an influential group active in its management, including Dr. Samuel Miller Brownell and Senator Gilbert E. Bursley, present Governor. These men believe that the Society could and should be made an effective channel for creating and maintaining a broad and vital interest in American history. One example of their efforts is this series of lectures on recent American Presidents. This is an important historical venture and one in which I am proud and honored to take part.

In tonight's talk on Dwight D. Eisenhower I must take a different approach from that which Professor Arthur Link used in his talk last year on Woodrow Wilson and from that which Professor Frank Freidel will probably use in his paper on Franklin Roosevelt next year. One reason is that I have come to my subject much more recently than either of them. Professor Link has devoted his whole professional career to the study of Woodrow Wilson. He has already completed five volumes of a massive biography and since 1954 has been working on a 40-volume edition of Wilson's writings. I started on my task of editing Eisenhower's private papers only a little over two years ago, so it would be presumptuous of me to attempt an analysis of the attitudes and ideas of President Eisenhower in the same way that Professor Link did here last year with those of President Wilson.

During these past two years I have concentrated on the compilation, selection, and annotation of Eisenhower's memoranda, directives, and correspondence written during the years of World War II. I do feel competent to speak as a professional historian about General Eisenhower. On the other hand, I know little more than any well informed citizen about President Eisenhower. Yet I am certain that Eisenhower's performance as President was closely connected to his performance as General. His experience during the war years prepared him for the tasks he had to face between 1953 and 1961. My purpose this evening is to consider how General Eisenhower's work affected that of President Eisenhower.

Let me begin this analysis of the relation of Eisenhower's training to his tasks by reminding you of the very formidable nature of his Presidential tasks. During the 1950's the 34th President of the United States had to face challenges as critical and as complicated as had any of his predecessors. These challenges were more external than internal. They involved diplomacy, grand strategy, and military organization. They required to a much lesser degree skills in handling political and economic matters which earlier Presidents needed to meet earlier challenges.

Not since the beginnings of the Republic had the United States faced such serious external threats. World War II left it the most powerful nation in the world and gave its citizens an awareness of global complexities and responsibilities. After 1945 the United States began to accept these new responsibilities by using its resources to revive the war-shattered economies of other nations West and East. It soon found itself called upon to mobilize a coalition of non-Communist nations against the threat of aggression by Communist Russia in the West and Communist China in the East.

The challenge of the Cold War intensified when Russia exploded an atomic bomb in 1949 and a hydrogen bomb in August, 1953, a few months after Eisenhower became President. It became even more serious when in October, 1957, the Soviets, by launching their satellite, demonstrated the capability of delivering nuclear warheads that could wipe out a large part of the United States in a matter of minutes. Never in its history had the nation felt itself in such peril of physical destruction. The only other super power in the world, ideologically dedicated to bringing down American values and its way of life, had the physical power to destroy its cities, its industries, and its defenses.

If the President's tasks were fundamentally different from those of the past century, so, too, was his training. Eisenhower had little direct involvement in party politics. Unlike his predecessors, he had never run for office before his first Presidential campaign. He knew little of the machinery or techniques of party politics or of the administration of political offices. Nor had he served, as had many of his predecessors, as a chief executive of one of the large industrial states. Except for Herbert Hoover and William Howard Taft, Americans had elected since the administration of General Grant either senators or governors as their Presidents. Both Taft and Hoover had served in important government posts and in a President's Cabinet before they reached the highest office in the land. If the challenges of the 1950's had been, as they were through most of American history, the reconciliation or protection of the interests of different geographical sections and economic classes in the face of changing social and economic conditions, then Eisenhower would have been only a little better prepared for the Presidency than General Taylor or General Grant. But the challenge was from without, not within. For this challenge Eisenhower's earlier experiences may have provided a far more valuable training than those of any senator or governor.

II

This training, it must be emphasized, was not that of a military officer as such, but rather the result of Eisenhower's specific experiences in World War II. These experiences trained him in three areas in which very few American military men had ever ventured before — the planning of global strategy, the creation of an Allied and unified command, and the conducting of diplomacy at the highest levels. These were new fields for American commanders precisely because World War II differed so radically from any other war the United States had fought.

Unlike the First World War the Second was truly a global war. In the First the fighting had been concentrated in Europe and after 1917 on the Western Front. In the Second there were always two and, during the American participation, three fronts in Europe. Simultaneously another great war was being fought in the Pacific. Therefore in World War II American military men had to think, for the very first time, about the realities of global strategy in terms of allocating limited available resources to different theaters of war in widely separated parts of the world.

For the first time, too, the Army and Navy fought under a single unified command. A large-scale unified operation by any modern military force had been attempted only once before, in the Gallipoli campaign of World War I, and it had ended in disaster. Moreover, by 1941 unified command involved not two but three services. The Air Force, which before 1918 was a romantic auxiliary, had in this country and in other nations developed its own tactics, strategy, esprit de corps, and approaches to war. Again, as was not true in World War I or in any earlier war, the high command in the Second War was a truly Allied one. In World War I Marshal Foch's overall command was only nominal. Indeed, he and the senior British, American, and French commanders — Haig, Pershing, and Petain — were together only once in the same room.

During World War II Eisenhower became intimately involved in both strategy and unified command. He played a critical role in the early definition of American global or grand strategy, and he created the largest and the most important allied, unified headquarters. This second task brought him in constant contact with the leaders of European nations and so developed his skill as a negotiator and diplomat. Of these three activities — grand strategy, command structure, and personal diplomacy — Eisenhower's initial training and initial testing came in the making of grand strategy. Indeed, it was his success in meeting this first test that opened the door to high command.

His opportunity came a week after the attack on Pearl Harbor, when George C. Marshall, the Army's Chief of Staff, ordered Eisenhower to Washington to take charge of war planning for the Far East and the Western Pacific. Marshall undoubtedly selected him because of the four years Eisenhower had spent in the Philippines with General Douglas MacArthur on a mission to build a Filipino Army. This experience not only made Eisenhower one of the best informed men about one major objective of the Japanese advance but it also won him the praises of General MacArthur. This younger subordinate, MacArthur reported, looked at military problems from the point of view of the high command.

During his first days in Washington Eisenhower threw

himself into planning for the Far East. At the same time, he was introduced to the making of strategy on a global level. He attended with General Marshall several of the conferences between Roosevelt and Churchill and the American and British Chiefs of Staff which were held in Washington in the first weeks of the war and which were known by the code name of *Arcadia.* There the two Allies reaffirmed the strategy of defeating Germany first. This strategy had been initially agreed upon when the Army and Navy staffs began late in 1940 to firm down plans to be used in case the United States was forced into the war. Its details were worked out with the British in conferences in early 1941. These plans to take the offensive in the Atlantic and the defensive in the Pacific had made Singapore the key to that defense.

The fall of Singapore, then, presented Eisenhower with his first critical challenge as a planner of grand strategy. The swift and completely unexpected collapse of that bastion in late January and early February forced a rethinking of all war plans. It caused many American newspapers and public figures, and some military leaders, too, to argue vehemently for putting Japan first. At the same time the brilliantly planned and executed Japanese advance was bringing desperate cries for men and equipment from commanders throughout the Western Pacific. The attempt to meet these many calls was resulting in a haphazard scattering of extremely limited American resources. Such continued misallocations of resources, Eisenhower feared, could bring a disaster that would affect far more than just the regions of his responsibility.

He outlined his answer to the crisis in a memorandum to Marshall, completed on February 28, entitled "Strategic Conceptions and Their Application to the Southwest Pacific." The paper began by pointing out that strategy in the Pacific could only be considered in relation to overall Allied global or grand strategy. It stressed that the logic of logistics reinforced the considerations of military strategy which had led Roosevelt, Churchill, and the Combined Chiefs of Staff of both nations to put Germany first. "To conduct a war in East Asia requires," he wrote, "for the same number of troops to be maintained there by the U.S. and Britain, at least three, possibly four times the shipping needed for a force of similar strength in the Atlantic," and shipping would long "remain the bottleneck of our effective effort."

The formulation of a strategy to permit an offensive in the West and an effective defense in the East required military planners, Eisenhower continued, "to differentiate sharply and definitely between those things whose accomplishment . . . is *necessary* to the ultimate defeat of the Axis powers, as opposed to those which are merely *desirable* because of their effect in facilitating such a defeat." Nothing should be allocated to the second category that might jeopardize the first. The necessary objectives were three: the maintenance of the United Kingdom, the retention of Russia in the war, and the prevention of the physical juncture of the Japanese and German forces in the India-Middle East area. Those objectives which were only desirable but not necessary were, in order of priority: the security of Alaska, the holding of bases south and west of Hawaii, the security of Burma, then of South America south of Natal, then of Australia, and then of bases on the West African coast.

To carry out the first of the three essential tasks — upholding England — priority must be given to planes and ships needed to keep the sea lanes open and to bring the life-giving supplies to Britain. The second — the support of Russia — called for, first, keeping up a maximum flow of lend-lease supplies and, second, for taking pressure off the Eastern front by beginning operations against northwestern Europe "sufficiently extensive in scale to engage from the middle of May onward, an increasing portion of the German Air Force, and by the late summer an increasing amount of his ground forces." As to India and the Middle East, Eisenhower insisted that the British must be responsible for the defenses there. Only after giving his analysis and answers to global or grand strategy did he outline a military strategy for the Southwest Pacific based on resources already in or on the way to the area.

From this memorandum grew, in time, the massive cross-Channel invasion of the Continent, the march across Europe to the Elbe, and the final victory over Germany. And in the long, complex, and circuitous story of the formulation and carrying out of this grand strategy Eisenhower played a continuing role. The first step came when Marshall, who had just promoted Eisenhower to head the War Plans Division, asked him to outline a scheme to carry out the part of his memorandum of February 28 which most critically affected the Army − that is, the cross-Channel attack on northwestern Europe. Eisenhower and his staff completed this plan by the end of March. Marshall and Franklin Roosevelt immediately approved it. The President then sent Marshall and Harry Hopkins to London, where they quickly won for it the backing of Churchill and the British Chiefs of Staff.

The plan as finally accepted had three parts. The code name *Bolero* was used to identify the initial build-up in Britain. *Sledgehammer* was the name for an emergency invasion to be launched across the Channel in the fall of 1942 if such an attack might be needed to prevent a Russian collapse or, as was most unlikely, if Germany became "critically weakened." Finally, *Round-up* was to be the major invasion in 1943.

As soon as he learned of its acceptance, Eisenhower moved quickly to put his plan into action. In May he visited England to review logistics and command structure as well as strategy and tactics. On his return Marshall, who had been increasingly impressed by Eisenhower's quick mind, his broad approach, and his willingness to take the initiative, passed over 366 more senior officers to make him Commander in Chief of the American Forces in the European Theater of War.

He had only just received his appointment, however, when Churchill personally concluded that *Sledgehammer* should be cancelled and an invasion of French North Africa be put in its place. The Prime Minister made a special trip to the United States to carry his argument to Roosevelt and the American Chiefs of Staff. Finally, in mid-July Roosevelt sent Marshall, Admiral Ernest J. King, and Harry Hopkins to London to confer with Eisenhower, Churchill, and the British Chiefs of Staff and to settle for once and for all Allied grand strategy for 1942 and 1943. The President instructed them to proceed with *Sledgehammer,* but if the British remained adamant, to develop a strategy that would have Americans fighting Germans before the end of 1942.

During these negotiations Eisenhower and his staff prepared daily an analysis of the American position. His concern and George Marshall's was that the substitution of a North African invasion (to be used only if its launching would help to keep Russia in the war) would delay the full-scale cross-Channel invasion until 1944 and that such a delay would be a serious blow to the Allied cause. But the British refused to change their stand. And since Roosevelt's instructions were clear, Marshall, Eisenhower, and the other Americans agreed with the British Chiefs of Staff that North Africa was a more promising alternative than Norway or the Middle East as the place where Americans would be fighting Germans in 1942.

Even after the decision for North Africa debate continued. The British and American Chiefs of Staff could agree on having Eisenhower command the invasion but disagreed over the location of the landings. The British wanted to land as far east as possible in order to secure the greatest military advantage from the move and so proposed the taking of Oran, Algiers, and even Bone, near the Tunisian border. The Americans preferred the less risky strategy of landing both inside and outside the Mediterranean at Oran and Casablanca. Eisenhower, who supported the British position, proposed a careful allocation of resources that convinced the Combined Chiefs of Staff of the possibility of reducing the forces planned for Algiers and Casablanca so as to permit landings at all *three* major ports and a follow-up landing at Bone.

Once the North African landings had been decided upon, Eisenhower's attention turned from grand strategy to command structure. He would again become involved in the planning of broad inter-theater strategy in the first part of 1944. But late in 1942 he had to concentrate on building a command to unify different services of different nations.

Eisenhower had already given much thought to command structure. He had listened at the *Arcadia* meetings to the debates over the merits of a unified command, which the Americans favored, and those of the committee system, which the British were used to. Eisenhower was given the task of drafting the directive for the first Allied unified command under General Archibald Wavell in the Far East. Both he and Marshall disliked the directive which he did compose because of its many "specific limitations" on the authority of the Supreme Commander. Yet they knew that such a directive gave such a commander as much authority as the nations involved were then willing to accept, and incidentally gave him far more power than Marshal Foch had had at the end of World War I. Eisenhower, too, had a chance to review the directives sent to Admiral Nimitz as commander of the Central Pacific theater and to General MacArthur as commander of the Southwest Pacific theater. Next he drafted what become his own directive when he went to London in June, 1942, which provided that "absolute unity of command should be exercised" over American land, sea, and air forces.

As soon as he received his appointment to command the North African landings, Eisenhower outlined to the British Chiefs the command organization that he desired. He wanted an Allied naval and an Allied air commander directly subordinate to him. Because ground forces were to make up the bulk of the attack, he asked to have both an American and a British army directly under him. He wanted his own staff to be fully integrated, that is, to be made up of officers from each of the three services of the two nations.

As the plans for the landings became more clearly defined, Eisenhower adjusted and modified his ideal structure to fit the needs of the three-pronged invasion and the follow-up drive to the east into Tunis under the command of the British General Kenneth A. N. Anderson. The real test of the British intentions came when they drafted their directive to Anderson, who was to have the major land role in the campaign, once the three ports were taken. On reading the proposed directive, Eisenhower immediately protested that it violated the principles of the unity of command. He was particularly disturbed by the statement that Anderson could report to the British War Office anytime he thought the British forces might be "imperilled." Instead, Eisenhower urged that the order "be deliberately written so as to emphasize the purpose of the U.K. and the U.S., to unify the Allied Force and to centralize responsibility for its operation, and that any authorization for departing from normal channels of command and communication should be made specifically dependent upon the rise of extraordinary and grave circumstances." The British complied handsomely. Anderson was to "carry out any orders issued" by his commanding general. "In the unlikely event" of receiving an order which he believed would "give rise to a grave and exceptional situation," he could appeal to the War Office, but only if he lost no opportunity nor endangered any part of the Allied Forces by so doing, and only if he first informed General Eisenhower.

On the whole the British had cooperated generously, and Eisenhower was certain that the results achieved had completely validated his faith in unified command. Early in January, after the weather and logistical ·difficulties halted Anderson's dash to the east, Eisenhower readjusted his command structure along centralized lines to carry out a more methodical advance into Tunis. He was, therefore, startled to learn that at the Casablanca conference in January, 1943, the Combined Chiefs of Staff, meeting with Roosevelt and Churchill, had turned away from the principle of unity of command. The reason was that the British wanted to continue the type of committee system that they had been using in the Mediterranean since the beginning of the war. The British argued that Sir Arthur Tedder, who headed the air forces, and Sir Harold Alexander, who controlled the land forces in the Middle East, and Sir Andrew Cunningham, who headed the naval forces in the North African landings, should command their respective services in the new Mediterranean theater. Eisenhower would then become essentially the chairman of this new committee. As General Alan Brooke, the Chief of the British Imperial Staff, noted in his diary: "We are pushing Eisenhower into the stratosphere and the rarified atmosphere of a Supreme Commander where he would be free to devote his time to political and inter-allied problems," and so leave military matters to the more experienced and in Brooke's opinion, more astute British commanders.

Eisenhower was dismayed when he learned of the new command structure. His own Chief of Staff had to talk him out of sending a sharp cable to the Combined Chiefs, insisting on a continuation of the organization that had worked so well in the initial North African landings. Eisenhower did, however, outline his views to Marshall in strong and clear terms. He then went on to achieve through his own efforts the very command structure that the Combined Chiefs had denied him in a formal directive. He accomplished this end in large part by the force of his own personality but partly also because his British commanders failed to agree on some critical strategic issues. He arranged for Tedder and Cunningham to set up their headquarters next to his in Algiers. Alexander, like Anderson before him, came to have charge of those land forces doing the actual fighting. Eisenhower kept in close touch with his army commanders by wire, phone, personal visits, and the exchange of staff officers. All three commanders were captured by Eisenhower's charm and still more by his honesty, fairness, and decisiveness. All three quickly became willing and loyal subordinates.

By September of 1943 Eisenhower had fashioned a command structure very similar to the one he had outlined as an ideal form to the British Chiefs in the previous August. The Combined Chiefs were impressed enough by his control of his forces and his ability to use them so that in August, 1943, they left to him full discretion as to when and where to make the attack on Italy. When in December, 1943, he was appointed Supreme Allied commander for the invasion of Europe, scheduled for the late spring of 1944, they let him create the type of command structure he wanted. It was, naturally, like the one he had developed in the Mediterranean. By then no one, not even General Alan Brooke, advocated a committee system of command.

In September, 1943, Lord Louis Mountbatten, who had just been appointed Supreme Commander of the Southeast Asia theater, wrote General Eisenhower for advice on creating a unified Allied command. In his reply the General stressed the importance of close personal relations as well as a clearly defined structure of authority and responsibility. The commanders and their integrated staffs must be physically located close to one another so that there would be constant personal contacts. However, "all communications to the Combined Chiefs of Staff must pass through you and no one else must be allowed to send communications to the Body." In addition, "final recommendations as to operations to be undertaken and requests for needed resources must likewise pass through you." Eisenhower ended the memorandum as he stated it: *The thing you must strive for is the utmost in mutual respect and confidence among the group of seniors making up the overall command . . . .* While the setup may be somewhat artificial, and not always so clean-cut as you might desire, your personality and good sense *must* make it work. Otherwise Allied action in any theater will be impossible." After the war Eisenhower recalled that: "The teams and staffs through which the modern commander absorbs information and exercises his authority must be a beautifully inter-locked, smooth working mechanism. Ideally the whole should be practically a single mind." Such an organization Eisenhower had come close to achieving by the spring of 1944. By the time he was ready to embark on one of the most massive military operations of all times, he had created the most effective unified, allied military organization of all times.

Valuable to Eisenhower's success in building a unified Allied command were his talents as a diplomat and negotiator. As he told Mountbatten, problems should never be approached on the basis of national interest alone. "An objective solution must be thought out and if your staff is divided functionally into its proper divisions and if each division contains able representatives from both nations, you will find the solution given to be objective and disinterested." This was always Eisenhower's approach even at the highest levels. His constant search for objective solutions to extremely complex and difficult problems between different nations made him one of the most effective diplomats in American history.

His first and continuing test as a diplomat came with the British. From the day he arrived in Great Britain in June, 1942, he was in constant contact with Winston Churchill and his leading ministers. In 1942 and again in 1944 Tuesday lunches and Friday dinners with the Prime Minister and weekend visits to Chequers became part of Eisenhower's normal routine. At these informal sessions and in larger conferences the two men discussed all the critical issues. For there were many genuine differences between the two allies.

Major issues included grand strategy as well as command structure. In general, the Americans favored a massive thrust to the industrial heart of Germany. The British preferred a peripheral strategy of hitting at weak points of Hitler's *Festung Europa*. On these questions the American general gained what he wanted without asking the British to sacrifice too much. For example, he prevented the Prime Minister from ordering what Eisenhower considered diversionary raids on the Aegean Islands. He obtained the invasion of southern France to support the main attack on Normandy in spite of Churchill's vehement opposition. He, too, overcame the Prime Minister's reluctance to giving him control of the Strategic Bombing Forces for the three months before and after the Normandy D-Day.

Lesser issues involved a complex of different matters such as amnesty orders, propaganda statements to Germany, censorship, bans on movements of diplomats, relations with the underground in occupation countries, and so on. These issues were often quite tricky and were potentially as divisive as the larger ones. For this reason Eisenhower maintained continuing discussions with the British leaders, even when decisions were not to be reached, in order to prevent unspoken biases and misinformation from creating misunderstandings.

The American commander needed even greater diplomatic skill in dealing with the French. Here the greatest problem was Charles de Gaulle. After the formation of the Committee of National Liberation in Algiers in June, 1943, De Gaulle became in actuality the head of the French state. This fact Franklin Roosevelt would not accept. The President's basic policy was that the government of liberated France should be formed only after the holding of free elections. He refused to give De Gaulle, whom he always distrusted, the advantage of pre-liberation recognition.

Roosevelt's adamant position greatly handicapped Eisenhower in his efforts to work out essential military and civil arrangements with the French. At least twice in 1943 Eisenhower prevented a disastrous break between Roosevelt and De Gaulle. The second time, he and his

Chief of Staff, General Smith, deliberately held up the delivery of a cable from Roosevelt to De Gaulle until advisers in Washington were able to get the President to modify and tone down the nature of his demands. In spite of the President's position, Eisenhower was able to reach informal agreements with General Pierre Koenig and more formal ones with De Gaulle himself to define the military relationship of the French forces fighting with the Allies and to carry out civil administration in liberated areas. After the invasion Eisenhower continued to negotiate with the French leader and his associates on many civil and military matters, including the liberation of Paris, the freeing of civilians, and the type of French currency to be issued.

There is not time here to consider Eisenhower's dealings with the representatives of the smaller occupied nations, nor his critical role in arranging the surrender of Italy and Germany and in the management of the affairs of these two nations after their surrender. Suffice it to say that from 1942 through 1945 Eisenhower was America's leading diplomat in Europe. Indeed, never before or since has an American had such close and continuous contact with European heads of state. Although his achievements were more those of a negotiator than a policy maker, in many cases the two roles were difficult to separate.

Lord Ismay suggested one reason for Eisenhower's success as a diplomat when he described him in his *Memoirs* as "tremendously alert, and seemed completely sure of himself; at the same time there was no trace of conceit or pomposity. Frankness, sincerity and friendliness were written all over him. But with it all, he was master in his own house, and he could be firm to the point of ruthlessness if the occasion demanded." Also in his diplomatic as well as military activities Eisenhower had the help of a devoted, hand-picked staff, headed by the brilliant, tough-minded Bedell Smith. As important, too, in diplomatic accomplishment was his commitment to working out an objective solution, his assumption that one could be found, and finally his willingness to agree to less than ideal terms and to accept fully the responsibility for his decisions.

III

I have discussed in some detail Eisenhower's work and contributions in the areas of grand strategy, command structure, and personal diplomacy during World War II. I have done this not only to indicate the type of training he received in these years but also to let you watch the man at work, handling complex and difficult affairs. For, as I have indicated, I can say much less about the way he approached his problems and arrived at decisions during the Presidential years. I can say more about what he did than how and why he did it.

Even the briefest consideration of Eisenhower's Presidency suggests that his World War II experience profoundly affected the way in which he met the awesome challenges of the 1950's. The relevance of the training to the task can be made particularly clear by reviewing Eisenhower's initial actions as President and then by examining his response to the hue and cry raised by the Soviet launching of the first satellite, Sputnik. (In this review all my quotations from Eisenhower come from his two-volume memoirs, *The White House Years.*)

On taking office in 1953 the new President immediately began to concern himself with grand strategy and with the command structure and personal diplomacy needed to carry it out. In his first message to Congress he stressed the need for a "coherent global policy." (I, 163) He fully accepted the basic bipartisan commitment of containing the aggressive and expansive tendencies of Russia and China. To keep this policy effective, he urged increased concentration on weapons development. For in 1953 as in 1942 weapons and their deployment played a critical role in the determination of grand strategy, but by 1953 these weapons had themselves greatly changed. He called again, as he had done earlier, for a setting of priorities as to goals and a careful allocation of resources in carrying them out. As a guide to determining these priorities he proposed placing "a greater reliance on deterrent nuclear weapons" and more effective air defense. (I, 175, 540)

Because of the tremendous destructive power of the new weapons, Eisenhower considered their control and limitation as an essential part of the new strategy. In April, 1953, he publicly outlined his program for international control of strategic materials and atomic energy as well as weapons. In December, at the opening of the first meeting of the United Nations General Assembly held during his Presidency, he presented an Atoms for Peace plan. He started discussions with the Russians on the possibilities of disarmament and began research which led to the Open Skies plan, which he proposed to the Soviets at Geneva in 1955.

In the first months of 1953 the new President also turned his attention to command structure. Despite the Unification Act of 1947, the three services were still pretty much going their own way, for that Act had given the new Secretary of Defense only the minimum of authority. He was permitted to coordinate but not to command the work of the three services. He could formulate only broad general policy but did not have administrative control. In other words, he was not to "run" the three services. While the revisions of the Act in 1949 had given the Secretary of

Defense a little more power, the Defense Department continued to be plagued with highly publicized inter-service rivalries and conflicts which could hardly have strengthened the nation's defenses. Less than a month after taking office, Eisenhower authorized a study of Defense Department reorganization. By June, 1953, Congress accepted his plans to strengthen the office of the Secretary of Defense "by establishing clearer lines of authority and responsibility," and "by eliminating unwieldy boards and committees and sub-stituting instead responsible executive officers." (I, 536) The second part of his program provided for the "mechanism of better strategic planning," by making the Joint Chiefs of Staff a planning rather than an executive agency and by increasing the chairman's powers. Eisen-hower's hope was that this would permit the JCS to seek and define national positions rather than merely to echo service ones. These moves reflect Eisenhower's earlier concern for a clear-cut command structure and for a greater unity of action and decision among the three services.

As necessary to the policy of containment as strategic plans for the employment and control of new weapons and an integrated and flexible defense establishment was the maintenance and strengthening of alliances and systems of alliances which the United States had arranged with non-Communist nations. Here Eisenhower relied heavily on personal diplomacy. During his first months in office he stayed in Washington while he was learning the intricacies of his new job. But soon he was making journeys to and receiving visits from the heads of other nations. In October, 1953, he travelled to the Mexican border to meet with President Ruiz Cortines. In November he spent three days in Canada conferring with its Prime Minister. In early

December he flew to Bermuda for a meeting with Winston Churchill and France's Premier, Joseph Laniel. "The sole object" of the last trip was, Eisenhower later wrote, "to provide friends in responsible positions an opportunity to meet and to talk more intimately about world problems than could be done through letters, telegrams, and special messengers." (I, 303) These talks were among the first of a total 210 personal meetings with heads of state or government which Eisenhower held during his Presidency.

The President's response to the launching of Sputnik in October, 1957, indicates even more clearly than his initial actions in office the importance of his World War II experience. Because Sputnik caught the American people unaware and because it dramatized the Soviets' ability to demolish American cities with rocket-delivered hydrogen bombs, it caused the nearest thing to an extended crisis during Eisenhower's term of office. The implications of Sputnik were underlined by a report on Russian capabilities made for the National Security council by a committee chaired by H. Rowan Gaither. This report stressed the large amount of resources the Russians were devoting to their armed forces and heavy industry. It warned of the Soviets' ability to launch by the end of 1959 an attack on the United States of a hundred InterContinental Ballistic Missiles carrying megaton nuclear warheads.

The President had a careful review made of grand strategy on the basis of the Gaither Report and its recommendations. After analyzing the many proposals offered, he approved of expanding the American ICBM program, begun in 1954, of increasing the number of the Strategic Air Command planes on alert, and of a further dispersion of SAC's bases. But he turned down the recommendation for a massive all-out bomb shelter program. On the whole, however, Eisenhower saw no reason to alter basic strategic plans and priorities because of a single Russian technological success, significant at it was. Although efforts along some lines had to be intensified, he believed that the United States should continue to have "both a sound defense and a sound economy—*if we set our priorities and stay with them.*" Some programs "were desirable but not essential," and would have to be reduced, but "we would not sacrifice security to worship a balanced budget." (II, 225) Eisenhower continued to approach the problems of grand strategy in 1957 as he had in 1942 by defining goals and objectives and then rationally allocating limited resources according to the priorities thus set.

Rather than fundamentally altering strategic plans and priorities, Eisenhower met the challenge pinpointed by Sputnik and the Gaither Report by improving the organization used to carry out the existing strategy and by relying on personal diplomacy to implement it. He proposed and Congress approved the formation of a new civilian agency—NASA—to conduct all non-military research in outer space. Of even more importance, Eisenhower seized this opportunity to achieve a genuine unified command structure for the nation's military forces—a goal which he had so long espoused. First, he recommended that the missile program be placed "under a single manager and administered without regard to the separate services." Next, he insisted upon a major reorganization of the existing military establishment, which would create unified commands in the field under the direct control of the President and the Secretary of Defense.

To achieve these ends he recommended to Congress in the spring of 1958 that all "deployed troops" be organized into "*truly* unified commands, all directly responsible to their designated commanders"; and that a "clear command channel" run directly from the President and the Secretary of Defense to the unified combatant commands. (II, 247-48) Neither the service Secretaries nor the service Chiefs were to be on the chain of command. Relieved of military responsibilities, the service Secretaries would concentrate on "managing the administration, training, and logistic functions of the services," while the Chiefs would continue in an advisory capacity as a planning staff. By an executive order he also abolished the JCS "committee system" of planning and instead set up a completely integrated staff in its place. In addition, he proposed that all defense research and development be placed under a single official reporting directly to the Secretary of Defense and also that Congress appropriate funds only to the Defense Department and not to the different services. Despite strong opposition within and without Congress, the Defense Reorganization Act, as passed in the summer of 1958, gave Eisenhower substantially all that he asked for. This Act, one of the most important in American military history, created a type of unified military establishment that Eisenhower had pioneered in building during World War II and had worked for in the years following the war. Its effectiveness is suggested by the very few changes that have been made in the nation's command structure since 1958.

The arts of diplomacy were as essential to discouraging a possible Russian attack as were clear-cut defense strategy and structure. Diplomacy was needed to keep the free world alliance strong and to convince the Russians of the folly of nuclear war. For a time, personal diplomacy had to wait. The passage through Congress of bills for military reorganization, for strengthening American education, and for intensifying research and development kept Eisenhower close to Washington during the spring and summer of 1958. Then came the fall mid-term elections. At the same time John Foster Dulles' prolonged illness forced the postponement of diplomatic planning.

In 1959, however, President Eisenhower turned to personal diplomacy in a way that no President has ever done before or since. That summer he flew to Europe to confer with Germany's Chancellor Adenauer, then with Prime Minister Harold MacMillan (who had been on Eisenhower's staff during the Mediterranean campaigns), and finally with Charles De Gaulle. Less than a week after his return he had long talks with Nikita Khrushchev in Washington and Camp David. In December came a journey to Italy, Turkey, Pakistan, India, Afganistan, Iran, Greece, Tunis, Morocco, France, and Spain. In February Eisenhower made a swing around South America. In May he was off to Portugal and France, and in June he flew to the Far East.

The purpose of these visits was much the same as those of his first overseas excursion in 1953. They were private, personal meetings, not formal summits. Consider how similar words describing these meetings are to those telling of his 1953 Bermuda trip. "Such talks were not expected to produce specific decisions; their real purpose was to facilitate an exchange of viewpoints and to sweep away some of the underbrush of misunderstanding that grows up when positive personalities communicate only through the written word and diplomatic channels." (II, 426, also 486) Yet important decisions were often reached. For example, Khrushchev in his meeting at Camp David agreed to remove the time limit the Russians had set for the signing of a Soviet-East Germany peace treaty and so make the future of Berlin a subject for negotiation and not unilateral action. In such conversations Eisenhower could use his charm and negotiating abilities to seek objective solutions which were as essential to the waging of peace as they had been a few years earlier to the somewhat less difficult task of waging war.

Eisenhower's training in personal diplomacy and his understanding of global strategy and command structure surely aided him in meeting the unprecedented challenges of the 1950's. Through his diplomacy he helped keep the NATO and other alliances firm, far firmer than they are today. Through personal contacts, too, he opened direct communications with the head of the Russian government for the first time since World War II. At the summit meetings at Geneva in 1955 and on Khrushchev's 1959 visit to the United States the heads of the two super-powers could agree that atomic war would be mutual suicide. While positive results of the meetings were disappointingly few, the critical beginnings of mutually satisfactory co-existence had begun. From these meetings came a cultural exchange program and in time a ban on nuclear testing.

Such a *detente* was encouraged by Eisenhower's constant watch over global strategy and military organization. American bases ringing Russia were kept manned and American soldiers and supplies kept abroad to bolster the defenses of our allies while a new arsenal of missiles was being developed. Throughout the two terms of his office American retaliatory power greatly exceeded Russian striking power. Under Eisenhower, too, the unification of the military services was finally achieved. Far less hampered by inter-service rivalries, the Defense Department was able to adjust its forces at home and abroad more quickly to meet the swiftly changing technological and strategic developments.

As a general in the 1940's, Dwight David Eisenhower proved his worth as a level-headed negotiator, a planner of grand strategy, and a creator of command structure. As President in the 1950's, he met the threat of unprecedented destruction without impairing democratic institutions and without violating basic American ideals and values. In meeting his tasks, I believe his training in strategy, structure, and diplomacy were of far more value than the more traditional presidential training in party politics, state government, or Congressional law-making.

DATE DUE

DEMCO 38-296